GOD'S PROMISES

For Every Believer to Live By

To encourage, strengthen, and give hope

ODELL YOUNG, JR.

SER ANTE
PUBLISHERS

Palmetto, GA • 30268

God's Promises for Every Believer to Live By
by Odell Young, Jr.
ISBN-13: 978-0615645100
ISBN-10: 0615645100
Printed in the United States of America

For Speaking Engagements, Book Orders, or additional information, contact Odell Young, Jr.:

Email: odell.youngjr@gmail.com
Call: 404-319-0913
Mail: P.O. Box 801
         Palmetto, GA. 30268

Dedication

Nothing gives me hope and inspiration like the promises of God. For His promises are His word and His word will stand forever. God's word is the most powerful thing in the universe and His promises are to encourage His followers.

I have studied and researched the promises of God for the past four years. I have come to the conclusion that the promises of God have been written in the bible for the believer to live a full life and experience the promises that God has made for every believer. Without the promises of God, we have nothing to hope or live for.

Everything that the believer will ever need or desire is contained in the promises of God. When God made man, He gave man an innate desire to depend on Him. No man can live without God, therefore God has made promises to His followers to show His love. God's requirement to the believer is to live a life that is pleasing and acceptable to His word, which is a reasonable price to pay for the promise of eternal life and all the other promises.

I realize that God wants the best for all of His children. However, He wants His children to obey His commandments and fear Him. This is the whole matter of man. I therefore dedicate this book to the following: God the Father, Jesus the Son and the Holy Spirit.

Contents

Acknowledgements

To Michael Coley, an apostle of God, and his family who reside in Olympia Fields, Illinois. Thank you Holy Spirit for sending Michael to share with me the secret things of God.

Introduction

GOD'S PROMISES

Through the following pages you will experience the heartfelt 'Love' of God through His promises that He made to His followers.

These promises contain every need and desire that every believer will ever hope for. God said there will be no wants in the life of His children.

The believer should make every effort to align his life according to God's word in order to receive the manifestation of the promises of God.

Worldly people (unbelievers) do not qualify for the promises of God. They must receive Jesus Christ as their Savior and Lord to benefit from God's promises.

All of God's promises will require a 'waiting' period. During this period of waiting, God will refine, train and mold the character of the believer to become more like Jesus.

In God's perfect timing, He will decide when a particular promise will be manifested in the believer's life. God requires that we trust Him even during our waiting for the promises that we desire to come to fruition in our lives. However, the promise will come in the life of the believer Because God will always keep His word. So, we should never stop believing in the promises of God.

The stories in this book are real and were witnessed by several of my close friends, my wife Delores, and myself. These stories are used to convey the power of God's promises when a believer calls on the name of Jesus when faced with trouble.

Psalm 91:14-16 (NIV) teaches us that *"Because He loves me, says the Lord, I will Rescue him; I will protect him for he acknowledges My name. He will call upon Me and I will answer him; I will be with him in trouble, I will deliver him and honor him. With long life I will satisfy him and show him My salvation."*

Introduction

In the book of Psalm, David said: *"I would have lost heart unless I had believed that I would see the goodness (promises) of the Lord in the land of the living.*(**Psalm 27:13**)

There are two kinds of promises in the scriptures; conditional and unconditional. The unconditional promises require nothing on behalf of the believer except to trust God. The conditional promises on the other hand, require some kind of performance from the believer.

God's promises are designed to give His followers hope, joy, peace, contentment and life. Let the promises of God take root in your heart and wait on Him; for then you are truly waiting on His very best. Our willingness to wait places a value on the promise that we are waiting for.

Some people have said that God is slow in manifesting His promises in the life of the believer. If there is a need to repent, it will delay the promises of God. The scripture teaches us; *"The Lord is not slack concerning His promise, as some count slackness, but is longsuffering toward us, not willing that any should perish but that all should come to repentance."* (**2 Peter 3:9**)

The greatest promise is stated in **John 3:16**; *"For God so loved the world that He gave His only begotten Son, that whoever believes in Him shall not perish but have eternal life."*

God wants His children to stand on His promises and refuse to be moved. The storms of life will come and the winds will blow, but if the believer would only stand firmly, the promise will be his in God's timing.

The intent of this book is to demonstrate the awesome value of God's promises to the believer and thusly, influence the believer to stand wholeheartedly on the promises of God.

In doing so, God will be glorified when the believer witnesses the manifestation of the promise that he is believing God for!

GOD'S PROMISES

The bible teaches us that God wants to give His children all things that are good for them. *"He Who did not spare His own Son, but delivered Him up for us all, how shall He not with Him also freely give us all things?"* (**Romans 8:32**)

The bible tells us in **2 Corinthians 1:20;** *"For all the promises of God in Him are yes, and in Him Amen, to the glory of God through us."*

The believer must continue to confess God's promises for his life and never lose hope. The promises will come if you continue to stand and not lose heart, because the promises are the word of God and He is faithful to give us the promise.

The scripture teaches us in the book of Hebrews; *"Let us hold fast the confession of our hope without wavering, for He Who promised is faithful."* (**Hebrews 10:23**)

The promises of God will never fail or become void, because God's word is sure and binding. We as believers must do our part and stay committed to God!

In **1 Kings 8:56** the bible tells us; *"Blessed be the Lord, Who has given rest to His people Israel, according to all that He promised. There has not failed one word of all His good promise, which He promised through His servant Moses."*

It is through God's divine power that He has made all things available to us through His precious promises.

As it is written; *"By which have been given to us exceedingly great and precious promises, that through these you may be partakers of the divine nature, having escaped the corruption that is in the world through lust."* (**2 Peter 1:4**)

Chapter One:

The Promise of Knowledge and Understanding

GOD'S PROMISES

THE PROMISE OF KNOWLEDGE

"Wisdom is the principal thing; therefore get wisdom." **(Proverbs 4:7)**

Wisdom has been personified as being present with God from the very beginning. The use of knowledge of God's word coupled with daily instructions from the Holy Spirit is the truest definition of wisdom.

The bible teaches us in Ecclesiastes 2:26:

"For God gives wisdom and knowledge and joy to a man who is good in His sight; but to the sinner He gives the work of gathering and collecting, that he may give to him who is good before God."

In James 1:5 it tells us;

"If any of you lacks wisdom, let him ask of God Who gives to all liberally and with reproach, and it will be given to him."

All of the promises of God are knowledge that the believer must study to show himself approved of them. When the believer knows the promises, he can stand on them for the desires of his heart. If the believer does not know the promises, he cannot benefit from them.

The bibles teaches in Hosea 4:6:

"My people are destroyed for the lack of knowledge."

The believer who does not have the knowledge and understanding of God's promises will therefore be destroyed.

The scripture teaches that; *"The fear of the Lord is the beginning of wisdom."* **(Proverbs 9:10)**

In Proverbs 12:1; we also learn that *"Whoever loves instruction loves knowledge."*

The Promise of Knowledge and Understanding

PRAYER OF THANKS FOR THE PROMISE OF WISDOM AND KNOWLEDGE

Father,

There is no other like You, and there will be no other like You in my life. You provide for Your children with love and mercy. My prayers are always answered by You and I can depend on Your every word and promise.

You make me wait in order to teach me to trust in You. You send me trials to increase my faith in You. You give me wisdom and knowledge to learn from You. I thank You for the promise of wisdom and knowledge, in the name of Jesus,

Amen.

The abundant life begins when the believer begins to seek the kingdom of God. The abundant life is having all the things God desires for the believer to have that are good for him.

The bible teaches us in **Matthew 6:33:** *"But seek first the kingdom of God and His righteousness, and all these things shall be added to you."*

A PROMISE OF A VICTORIOUS LIFE

As it is written; *"Yet in all things we are more than conquerors through Him (Christ) Who loved us."* **(Romans 8:37)**

In time, the believer will know and understand that there is power in being one with Christ; for He is the One Who gives the believer strength to do all things that are within the will of God.

Jesus has overcome the world and in Him, we have victory in all that we do. All things are subject to God; for He made all things through Himself and without Him nothing was made that was made.

GOD'S PROMISES

The scripture teaches us that the believer who believes and trusts in the Lord has within him Christ, Who is greater than he (Satan) who rules the earth.

We are now the servants of righteousness and not the servants of sin.

"O Death, where is your sting?O Hades, where is your victory? The sting of death is sin, and the strength of sin is the law. But thanks be to God, Who gives us the victory through our Lord Jesus Christ. **(1 Corinthians 15:55-57)**

A PROMISE OF DELIVERANCE

Jesus has made a promise to the believer that He would deliver the believer from the wrath of God. The scripture teaches us; *"For God so loved the world that He gave His only begotten Son, that whoever believes in Him should not perish but have everlasting life."* **(John 3:16)**

God has made a way for every born again believer to live eternally with Him in heaven. The believer does not have to be concerned about the wrath of God that will come upon the unbeliever.

"And to wait for His Son from heaven, Whom He raised from the dead, even Jesus who delivers us from the wrath to come." **(1 Thessalonians 1:10)**

The scripture teaches us that the punishment for sin is death. But Jesus has paid the price of sin for all believers.

The bible teaches us what God will do for the believer whose heart of love is set toward God. In **Psalm 91:14,** it tells us *"Because he has set his love upon Me, therefore I will deliver him; I will set him on high, because he has known My name."*

The Promise of Knowledge and Understanding

KNOWLEDGE WILL KEEP THE BELIEVER FROM

BEING DESTROYED

The bible teaches us in the book of Hosea that without knowledge, the people of God will be destroyed.

"My people are destroyed for the lack of knowledge." (**Hosea 4:6**)

God wants the believer to study to show himself approved of Him. If we do not study God's word, we will not know His commandments and His decrees in order to obey Him. When the believer does not study God's word, he is in essence rejecting the knowledge of His kingdom.

God wants to reveal the secret things of His kingdom to the believer. This can only be accomplished by studying God's word, seeking Him and making a total commitment to Him.

The believer must also develop a relationship with the Holy Spirit that will guide him into all truths of God's word. The word of God is alive and the believer will get the knowledge through the leading of the Holy Spirit.

God desires for His children to get knowledge so that they can have understanding. It is knowledge that gives us wisdom and understanding. God's word will give us wisdom, if we are walking in the Spirit. It is the Spirit of God that will reveal wisdom to the believer.

The scripture warns us not to reject knowledge (God's word). In the book of Hosea it tells us: *"Because you have rejected knowledge, I also will reject you from being priest for Me. Because you have forgotten the law of your God, I also will forget your children"* (**Hosea 4:6b**)

The Holy Spirit will relate the things He has heard from God and God will reveal these things to the believer as he studies the word of God.

Remember, God speaks to the believer through His word and the Voice that is speaking to us is the Holy Spirit. Without the Holy Spirit, there would be many things in God's word we would not understand.

The Holy Spirit is our helper and is always there to help us understand God's word. We should always seek God for help through the Holy Spirit to bring understanding in all scripture. God will do just that because He wants us to get the spiritual understanding of His word.

THE BELIEVER WILL RECEIVE IN PROPORTION TO HIS GIVING

The scripture teaches us that we shall reap what we sow. When we give much, we will receive much and when we give a little, we will receive a little.

The book of Corinthians tells us:

"But this I say; he who sows sparingly will also reap sparingly, and he who sows bountifully will also reap bountifully." **(2 Corinthians 9:6)**

"Give, and it will be given to you; good measure, pressed down, shaken together, and running over will be put into your bosom. For with the same measure that you use, it will be measured back to you." **(Luke 6:38)**

Chapter Two:

The Promise of Hope

GOD'S PROMISES

A PROMISE OF HOPE AND A FUTURE

God has not only made provision of a future for the believer, but also hope. The believer's hope should be in the word of God. However, God knows how to sustain the hope that is within the believer.

Without hope in the life of anyone, there is little anticipation of living a productive life. Therefore, God has given the believer provision for hope.

"For I know the thoughts I think toward you, says the Lord, thoughts of peace and not of evil, to give you a future and a hope." (**Jeremiah 29:11**)

All of God's children need hope and a future. This is a message that the pastor should major on when he is preparing his sermon to young people in the church.

If the pastor does not reach the young people with a message of hope and a future, the church will eventually lose them. Most of the young members will lose interest and drift away. Consequently, the church will lose its future members and experience suffering!

"But those whose hope in the Lord will renew their strength. They will soar on wings like eagles; they will run and not grow weary, they will walk and not be faint," because their hope is in the Lord. (**Isaiah 40:31, NIV**)

"Now may our Lord Jesus Christ Himself, and our God and Father, Who has loved us and given us everlasting consolation and good hope by grace, comfort your hearts and establish you in every good word and work." (**2 Thessalonians 2:16-17**)

The Promise of Hope

A Prayer of Thanks for
The Promise of Hope and Future

Father,

Our hope is in You alone. No wonder we are happy in the Lord, for we are trusting in Him. We trust His holy name. Yes, Lord let Your constant love surround us. I thank You for this promise of hope and a future.

Amen.

God only gives us things that are in accordance to His will. If we desire something that is not good for us, He will not give it to us. Why, because God knows the future and when a desire that we ask for is not good for us in the future, He will not honor it. He loves us so much that He will even protect us from ourselves.

A Promise To Receive The Desires Of The Heart

It pleases God to give His children good things when they are obedient to His commandments. God knows how to give better gifts to His children compared to gifts earthly fathers give to their children.

The scripture teaches us in **Matthew 7:11;** *"If you then, being evil know how to give good gifts to your children, how much more will your Father Who is in heaven give good things to those who ask Him."*

God always knows the needs and the desires of His children. It gives God pleasure to give His children their desires when their desires line up with the will of God.

The Lord is always near to those who call on Him. The scripture teaches us that whatever we ask God for according to His will, we must believe that we have received it and it will be ours. Thus, if we believe He hears us, whatever we ask for will be ours. The key to God's promises is to believe.

Every human being on the face of the earth has desires. Some desires are small and some are large. The size of the desire does not matter to God. It is the faith behind the desire that is important to God. The bible teaches us that those who come to God must believe.

Hebrews 11:6 states; *"But without faith it is impossible to please Him, for he who comes to God must believe that He is, and that He is a rewarder of those who diligently seek Him."*

Desires are a part of the human existence. For God made man and gave him desires and the capacity to hope. Our hope is based on our desires. Without hope, there is no real basis to live. The incentive to live is based on our desires, our hopes, and our loved ones. God, in His infinite wisdom, is aware of all of our hopes and wishes. He knows everything we are hoping for and everything that is good for us. God only wants the best for His children and He knows that sometimes what the believer wants may not be the best for them.

The bible teaches in **Matthew 6:33:** *"But seek first the Kingdom of God and His righteousness, and all these things shall be added to you."*

What are these things? All the things that are good for you that are within God's will and the things that are necessary for you to perform the assignment God has for you which is your purpose for life.

God wants His children to be delighted in His commandments and be committed to the things of God.

The scripture teaches us in **Jeremiah 1:5;** *"Before I formed you in the womb I knew you."*

I believe that at the time of conception, God molded us just as a potter molding clay to become a masterpiece for future use to glorify the Maker.

God gave each person a purpose to fulfill on this earth. At the same time, He placed desires and dreams into the making of everyone. Some people discover their dreams and desires early in life, while others discover them later in life.

There are people who never discover their true self, which contains their purpose, dreams, and desires. I believe that once a person begins to seek God, these things will be discovered. Whether he does anything about them is another story.

God only desires the best for His children, and some of the desires that the believer has may not be good for him. Therefore, God will not allow that desire to manifest in the believer's life.

The bible teaches us that God has given the believer some of His attributes. In **Genesis 1:26** it says; *"Let Us make man in Our image, according to Our likeness; let them have dominion over the fish of the sea, over the birds of the air, and over the cattle, over all the earth and over every creeping thing that creeps on the earth."* Because we have some of the attributes of God, we can do more than we think we can do!

When God speaks, things happen, and things are created. In **Genesis 1:3** God said, *"Let there be light; and there was light."*

The bible teaches us to imitate God as dear children. Children will naturally imitate their parents when they are little. **Ephesians 5:1** tells us, *"Therefore be imitators of God as dear children."*

Romans 4:17b tells us, *"God, Who gives life to the dead and calls those things that do not exist as though they did."*

God wants to give His children all things that are good for them in His sight. The believer will never get any desire from God that will prove detrimental in his future. We do not know what is always good for us, but God does. Therefore, God may not give all that we ask.

God wants His children to trust Him and be obedient to His word. God does not want to hold back on a believer, but He does require the believer to wait on the promises. God desires a relationship with every believer that will require refining and molding of his character. The fruit of the Spirit is an example of the character that God wants for every believer.

The believer who delights himself in the Lord and in His commands will receive all the blessings and promises that God has. The scripture teaches us in the book of Psalm to *"Delight yourself also in the Lord, and He shall give you the desires of your heart."* **(Psalm 37:4)**

According to scripture, the believer can have what he says if the thing that he says is in the will of God. If what he says does not line up with the will of God, He does not hear us. If God does not hear the believer, He will not get the thing he is seeking. However, God will determine when we will receive His promises. Be assured, they will come in time.

In **Mark 11:23** it says; *"For assuredly, I say to you, whoever says to this mountain, be removed and cast into the sea, and does not doubt in his heart, but believes that those things he says will be done, he will have whatever he says."*

What desires? The desires that God has placed on the inside of the believer and those desires that the believer has that are good for him in God's view.

A True Story: The Favor of God

Sarah was busy cleaning her home when she happened to see a man walk pass the bay window of the living room toward the left side of the house. She looked to the right side of the house to see the kind of truck parked in the driveway. It was a gas company truck. It suddenly dawned on her that she had forgotten to pay the past due bill. Sarah began to pray and ask God for favor with the gas company so that they would not turn off the gas. About three minutes later the doorbell rang. The man from the gas company came to the door and said; "I am here to turn off your gas, however, I'll give you time to go and pay your bill. I'll make your house the last one on my list today and come back later. That way your gas will not have to be turned off."

Sarah said praise the Lord and thanked the man. She called her husband and told him what had happened. She then left to go and pay the bill. Sarah knew that God had answered her prayer, and intervened to prevent the disconnection of her gas.

A Promise Of Joy And Happiness

"But rejoice to the extent that you partake of Christ's sufferings, that when His glory is revealed, you may also be glad with exceeding joy." **(1 Peter 4:13)**

The joy that comes from the Lord to the believer is not temporary. It is promised to last for the life of the believer and will extend into eternity.

We are happy when we are learning, growing and accomplishing things in our life that line up with the will of God. We should always be working toward the dreams and desires that have been placed in us by God.

Remember, we are the clay and God is the Potter Who made us. He is the only one Who knows what will give us complete happiness and satisfaction.

When we are operating in the purpose He made us, we are at the maximum point of happiness. It is impossible for a believer to do something that is outside of the purpose God made him and be completely happy in the long run.

When the believer does not know his purpose, he should seek God for the answer. He can also go to Matthew 6:33 and seek the answer in the word of God.

"But seek first the kingdom and His righteousness, and all these things (your purpose) shall be added to you." **(Matthew 6:33)**

A Prayer of Thanks for
The Promise of Joy and Happiness

Father,

I delight in doing Your will for my life. I will keep Your word close to my heart to please You. Who shall separate my Love for You? You have loved me from the time I was formed in my mother's womb; You provided for every need that I had, even when I was lost and living in darkness. You give my heart joy and happiness. My soul longs for Your presence and I thank You for the promise of joy and happiness, in the name of Jesus.

Amen.

A Promise Of Peace

The scripture teaches us that peace is one of the fruits of the Spirit. This means that peace cannot come from the world. One must be led by the Spirit and not walk according to the flesh to receive peace. As the believer is abiding in God and the word of God is abiding in the believer, his mind will remain on God. Then there will be peace that is beyond understanding in the life of the believer.

The scripture teaches us in **Isaiah 26:3**:

"You will keep him in perfect peace, whose mind is stayed on You, because he trusts in You."

There is always peace beyond our understanding when we keep our focus on God. The believer should never focus on his problems or any burden that he may have.

Jesus said to bring all of our burdens and leave them with Him. The bible teaches us to pray about everything and worry about nothing.

Philippians 4:6-7 tells us: *"Be anxious for nothing, but in everything, by prayer and supplication, with thanksgiving, let your request be known to God; and the peace of God, which surpasses all understanding, will guard your hearts and minds through Christ Jesus."*

God wants to give the believer every request that he asks for that is good for him in God's view. God will never give a believer any request that may be harmful later in life. God is concerned about the future of every believer.

The bible teaches us that God is responsible for the believer's future. **Jeremiah 29:11** tells us; *"For I know the thoughts I think toward you, says the Lord, thoughts of peace and not of evil, to give you a future and a hope."*

God will not only give peace to His children who love Him; the scripture teaches us that He will give His children 'great peace'.

"Great peace have those who love Your law. And nothing causes them to stumble." **(Psalm 119:165)**

"The Lord will give strength to His people; the Lord will bless His people with peace." **(Psalm 29:11, NUJV)**

The scripture teaches; *"But the meek will inherit the land and enjoy great peace."* **(Psalm 37:11, NIV)**

THE BELIEVER SHOULD LIVE A LIFE OF CONFIDENCE

It is never wise to do anything in our own power without acknowledging the direction of the Holy Spirit to guide us and give us confidence.

The scripture teaches us in **Proverbs 3:5-6;** *"Trust in the Lord with all your heart, and lean not on your own understanding; in all your ways acknowledge Him, and He shall direct your paths."*

Our confidence should always be in Christ Jesus and not in ourselves. For without Jesus we cannot accomplish anything. He is the center of the believer's life. He is our strength and our hope.

In the book of **John 15:5,** the scripture teaches us; *"I am the Vine, you are the branches. He who abides in Me, and I in him, bears much fruit; for without Me you can do nothing."*

The bible teaches us to never rely on our own understanding, for God wants us to do everything in the power and might of His Son Jesus Christ.

"For the Lord will be your confidence, and will keep your foot from being caught." **(Proverbs 3:26)**

This scripture should be the basis of the confidence that the believer should live by on a daily basis:

"I can do all things through Christ Who strengthens me." **(Philippians 4:13)**

Even our boldness should not be in ourselves but in the confidence of the word of God. In the book of **Ephesians 3:12** it tells us; *"In Whom we have boldness and access with confidence through faith in Him."*

When we keep our minds stayed on the Lord, He will guide and direct us to always do His will each step of the way.

"Beloved, if our heart does not condemn us, we have confidence toward God." **(1 John 3:21)**

The believer should display confidence in himself with a consciousness of the One Who lives on the inside of him, that is Jesus Christ, our Savior. He will give the believer strength to do all things. Life is not easy and the bible does not say it is easy. However, with Jesus living on the inside of us, we can be overcomers and conquerors in everything that we do.

We will need strength on a daily basis and God has promised us that He will give us strength when we ask Him.

The unbeliever has separated himself from God, therefore he cannot ask God for anything and expect to receive it. He is not a child of God until he accepts Jesus as his Savior and Lord.

A Promise To The Believer To Have What He Confesses

The bible teaches us that the power of God is working in the believer when the believer is abiding in God and the word of God is abiding in the believer. He has power that has been bestowed upon him in the name of Jesus.

GOD'S PROMISES

The scripture teaches us in **Ephesians 3:20;** *"Now to Him Who is able to do exceedingly abundantly above all that we ask or think, according to the power that works in us."*

The power that works in us is the power that is given to the believer from God Himself. This same power enables the believer to be an overcomer and do the will of God.

This same power also extends into other areas of the believer's life because he is a son of God. The bible teaches us that this power can work in the believers life to have what he says if what the believer says is in line with the will of God.

The scripture teaches us that through faith in God, we can have what we say. In the book of **Mark 11:23** it tells us; *"For assuredly I say to you, whoever says to this mountain, 'Be removed and be cast into the sea,' and does not doubt in his heart, but believes that those things he says will be done, he will have whatever he says."*

God has placed desires in the hearts of His children and it is these desires that gives us hope. It is this hope that gives the believer the desire to live for God. Without Jesus, there is no real hope for the believer to live, because He is the source of our life.

The Spirit of Truth lives on the inside of the believer which is the Spirit of God and encourages the believer to live in a way that pleases God. The believer does not live to please himself, but to please God his Savior. It is this commitment that the believer has made to God that will allow God to be pleased to call the believer a son.

It pleases God to see His children prosper in everything that they do when the believer places God first in everything that he does.

Chapter Three:

The Promise to Reward

A Promise To Reward The Believer

According to God's promises the believer has many rewards in store from God Himself. It gives God pleasure to reward His children. It also gives God pleasure to see His children prosper.

Jesus wants the believer to ask Him for the things he desires. For God is glorified when the believer receives from Him.

"But love your enemies, do good, and lend, hoping for nothing in return; and your reward will be great, and you will be sons of the Most High. For He is kind to the unthankful and evil." **(Luke 6:35)**

"The Lord repay your work, and a full reward be given you by the Lord God of Israel, under Whose wings you have come for refuge." **(Ruth 2:12)**

Every believer who diligently seeks God is promised a reward:

"But without faith it is impossible to please Him, for he who comes to God must believe that He is, and that He is a rewarder of those who diligently seek Him." **(Hebrews 11:6)**

The believer who is doing the work of God which includes feeding the poor, sheltering destitute people, caring for orphans and widows and preaching the gospel, will be rewarded by God. These are the services of God and the believer who desires to please God should help in at least some of the ways mentioned above. God loves mankind and He wants His children to have their basic needs met. The believer is God's partner here on earth and He expects us to help and assist those who cannot help themselves.

In **Psalm 41:1-4** it says; *"Blessed is he who considers the poor; The Lord will deliver him in time of trouble. The Lord will preserve him and keep him alive, And he will be blessed on the earth; You will not deliver him to the will of his enemies. The Lord will strengthen him on his bed of illness; You will sustain him on his sickbed. I said, 'Lord be merciful to me; heal my soul, for I have sinned against You."*

The things that we perform for those in need will last forever according to the word of God. The bible speaks of a reward for performing this service of God. It is a crown, and the bible refers to it as a crown that is imperishable. It is a reward that the world cannot give because it is eternal.

The scripture teaches us; *"If anyone's work which he has built on it endures, he will receive a reward."* (**1 Corinthians 3:14**)

God has many rewards in store for the believer who is helping the poor and doing the work of God. It gives God pleasure to reward His children when they are obedient. God is glorified when the believer receives the things they desire through Jesus Christ. God wants the believer to love his enemies and lend to those who have a financial need.

THE BELIEVER CAN DO ALL THINGS THROUGH CHRIST

The scripture teaches us that nothing is impossible to those who believe in Jesus. Jesus is our strength and our source for everything! We must always abide in Him and He in us. We can be very productive when we include Jesus in every aspect of our life. When we abide in Him, we are making Him our partner in life.

The bible tells us that everything was made by Him. With His help, as His partner we can do all things within His will.

In **Philippians 4:13** the scripture teaches; *"I can do all things through Christ Who strengthens me."*

Jesus said that the believer can do the things He did on earth and even greater things because He was to going to His Father.

"Most assuredly, I say to you, he who believes in Me the works that I do he will do also, and greater works than these he will do, because I go to My Father." (**John 14:12**)

GOD'S PROMISES

THE BELIEVER IS PROMISED TO RULE THE WORLD

In every believer's life, God has placed an abundance of power to do great things. Without this 'God-given' power, we cannot do anything worth noting.

In order for the believer to make it in the earth, there must be power. This power must come from God. God is the giver of power in the life of the believer to accomplish great things. We are like God in some aspects.

We are to rule over the earth just like God rules over the universe. God has given the believer the power to speak and change or create things on this earth if he has the faith. This power to speak is illustrated in several places in the scriptures.

THE AGREEMENT OF TWO BELIEVERS
WILL BE GRANTED

There is power in an agreement when there are two believers asking God for anything. The bible tells us when two or three gather in His name, He is there in the midst. Only two people are necessary to agree on anything that is asked of God and He will grant their request.

"Again I say to you that if two of you agree on earth concerning anything that they ask, it will be done for them by My father in heaven." **(Matthew 18:19)**

The Promise to Reward

A Promise To Strengthen The Believer

"Be of good courage, and He shall strengthen your heart, all you who hope in the Lord" **(Psalm 31:24)**

God has promised to give strength to the believer when he is weak. God never changes. He gave strength to the people of Israel to make them strong at the exact moment they needed it.

"Oh God, You are more awesome than Your holy places. The God of Israel is He Who gives strength and power to His people. Blessed be God!" **(Psalm 68:35)**

Chapter Four:

The Promise that God Will Lead You

GOD'S PROMISES

A Promise To Receive The Holy Spirit

The very last promise Jesus made to His disciples can be found in **Luke 24:48-49(NIV)**: *"You are witnesses of these things. I am going to send you what my Father has promised; but stay in the city until you have been clothed with power from on high."*

After the promise of the Holy Spirit, Jesus led the disciples out of the city of Bethany. Jesus lifted up His hands to bless the disciples; and He was taken up into heaven. Jesus promised before He left the earth that He would send the Comforter (the Holy Spirit).

The Comforter would not come unless Jesus left the earth. The Comforter will guide the believer into all truth. He would speak only what He hears, and He will bring glory to Jesus **(John 14:16)**.

Before Jesus left the earth, He told the disciples that they would see Him again.

Ephesians 1:13 tells us; *"In Him you also trusted, after you heard the word of truth, the gospel of your salvation; in whom also, having believed, you were sealed with the Holy Spirit of promise."*

God sent His Son Jesus to the world to die for the sins of many and to redeem His children.

In Galatians, it tells us that Christ redeemed us in order; *"that the blessing of Abraham might come upon the Gentiles in Christ Jesus, that we might receive the promise of the Spirit through faith."* **(Galatians 3:14)**

The believer who is controlled by the Holy Spirit thinks about the things that pleases the spirit. By letting your natural mind control you will lead to death. But letting the Spirit control your mind will lead to life and peace.

The Promise that God Will Lead You

Once we have the Holy Spirit living in us, it gives us a sense of purpose and direction. We are not prone to waste our time and skills, but rather reach out to others who are lost.

The mission of the Holy Spirit is to help the believer and comfort him with a seal until the day of redemption. The Holy Spirit will also help us live the christian life and help us understand the word of God. Without the help of the Holy Spirit, the believer cannot live the Christian life.

"If you then, being evil, know how to give good gifts to your children, how much more will your heavenly Father give the Holy Spirit to those who ask." **(Luke 11:13)**

"Now may the God of hope fill you with all joy and peace in believing, that you may abound in hope by the power of the Holy Spirit." **(Romans 15:13)**

A PROMISE TO RECEIVE THE KINGDOM OF GOD

It is the desire of God to give the kingdom of God to His children. We will receive the kingdom of God by seeking the kingdom of God and this is a promise of God Himself.

The scripture teaches us in **Luke 12:31-32**: *"But seek the kingdom of God, and all these things shall be added to you. Do not fear little flock, for it is your Father's good pleasure to give you the kingdom."*

The bible defines the kingdom of God as: *"For the kingdom of God is not eating and drinking, but righteousness and peace and joy in the Holy Spirit."* **(Romans 14:17)**

God wants to lead His children by the Holy Spirit. The Holy Spirit does not speak on His own account but rather speaks on the things that He has heard from the Father. The Holy Spirit is like a mouthpiece of God.

GOD'S PROMISES

A PROMISE TO BE LED BY THE HOLY SPIRIT

All believers will need to be led from time to time in their walk with God. We will be faced with many crossroads and detours that will have to be reckoned with.

Many times the believer may be faced with something that appears to be the truth but is not exactly true. The believer can always get help by seeking the Holy Spirit.

"However, when He, the Spirit of truth, has come, He will guide you into all truth; for He will not speak on His own authority, but whatever He hears He will speak; and He will tell you things to come." (**John 16:13**)

A PROMISE TO KNOW THE TRUTH

"We are of God. He who knows God hears us; he who is not of God does not hear us. By this we know the spirit of truth and the spirit of error." (**1 John 4:6**)

"Nevertheless I tell you the truth. It is to your advantage that I go away; for if I do not go away, the Helper will not come to you; but if I depart, I will send Him to you." (**John 16:7**)

"Now hope does not disappoint, because the love of God has been poured out in our hearts by the Holy Spirit who was given to us." (**Romans 5:5**)

"Or do you not know that your body is the temple of the Holy Spirit Who is in you, Whom you have from God, and you are not your own." (**1 Corinthians 6:19**)

The Promise that God Will Lead You

A Promise To Those Who Consider The Poor

God has promised blessings to those who consider the poor; and according to the bible, the poor will always be with us. However, God is concerned about their welfare and needs. So God promises a reward to those who consider the poor.

The scripture tells us that those who aid the poor will be blessed by God in several ways: They will be strengthened on their sick bed and protected from their enemies. The other promises are deliverance and preservation of life.

"Blessed is he who considers the poor; The Lord will deliver him in time of trouble. The Lord will preserve him and keep him alive, and he will be blessed on the earth; You will not deliver him to the will of his enemies. The Lord will strengthen him on his bed of illness; You will sustain him on his sickbed." **(Psalm 41:1-3)**

A Promise Of A Hundredfold

For the believer who has left (loss) anything to follow Jesus, he will receive back to him a hundredfold. Many believers have lost material possessions to follow the teachings of Christ. They have given up things that they worked hard for in order to do the work God has called them to do.

God has said in His word that He would multiply the value of their loss and they would inherit eternal life.

"And everyone who has left houses or brothers or sisters or father or mother or wife or children or lands for my name sake; shall receive a hundredfold, and inherit eternal life." **(Matthew 19:29)**

GOD'S PROMISES

A Promise To The Believer To Bear Much Fruit

The bible teaches us that if we abide in Jesus, we will bear much fruit (have a productive life).

In **John 15:5** the scripture tells us; *"I am the Vine, you are the branches. He who abides in Me, and I in him, bears much fruit; for without Me you can do nothing."*

Bearing much fruit is synonymous to being successful. God has placed intrinsic desires in each one of us to achieve something in life. Everything that is necessary to achieve is already in us, but it is God Who gives the power to make it happen. In other words, we can plant and water a seed that is placed in the soil of the ground, but only God can make it grow.

Our success in anything will depend on God's help. The bible teaches us that we can do nothing on our own. For without God we have no power or strength. He is the source of everything to the believer. Our body operates the way it does because God has designed it to function in an autonomous manner even when we are asleep.

We can be successful in the things we desire to do if we obey God and ask for His help.

In the book of **Mark 11:24,** Jesus makes us a promise: *"Therefore I say to you, whatever things you ask when you pray, believe that you receive them and you will have them."*

God has given us a body that He designed to accomplish countless things in life. The believer must rely and trust in God to maximize his full potential.

The scripture teaches us in **Psalm 139:14,** *"I will praise You for I am fearfully and wonderfully made."*

The Promise that God Will Lead You

The believer must also remember that God was not made to serve us, but we were made to serve God and others. When we serve others who cannot help themselves, we are serving God. The scripture tells us to serve the poor, the homeless, the destitute, the sick, the orphans, and widows. When we serve them, God will reward us and bless us according to His word.

A Promise To Honor The Believer

The bible teaches us that the harvest is plentiful, but the laborers are few. There is much work to do in the body of Christ. God loves the poor, the needy, and the destitute. When we serve them, we are expressing our love to the Father.

The scripture tells us in John; *"If anyone serves Me, let Him follow Me; and where I am, there My servant will be also. If anyone serves me, him my Father will honor."* **(John 12:26)**

Chapter Five:

The Promise of a New Life

GOD'S PROMISES

WORDS SPOKEN BY THE BELIEVER

WILL BE HEARD BY ANGELS

The scripture teaches us that faith is the factor that gives our words power to do certain things in life. However, what we are speaking to change or create must be in God's will. Every believer must speak only the things he wants to live within his life. The bible teaches us to ask for what we want and do not speak of what we do not want. Our words have more power than we think. We must pay close attention to what we say and what we think. Our spoken words have the power to create or destroy when they are spoken with conviction and authority.

In Luke 17, the writer is referring to a mulberry tree, which is symbolic of a circumstance or a condition in the believer's life.

It is written:

"So the Lord said, 'If you have faith as a mustard seed, you can say to the mulberry tree, Be pulled up by the roots and be planted in the sea,' and it would obey you." **(Luke 17:6)**

"For assuredly, I say to you, whoever says to this mountain, 'Be removed and be cast into the sea,' and does not doubt in his heart, but believes that those things he says will be done, he will have whatever he says." **(Mark 11:23)**

The Promise of a New Life

A Promise To The Believer Who Obeys

The Word Of God

God will always honor the obedience of His saints, because He knows that the blessings He has for them begins with obedience. Disobedience in the life of the believer will cease all blessings from God.

The scripture teaches us in Leviticus 26:3-4:

"If you walk in My statutes and keep My commandments, and perform them, then I will give you rain in its season, the land shall yield its produce, and the trees of the field shall yield their fruit."

The believer should always remember that obedience and disobedience have consequences. One will bring blessings and the other will bring chastisement from God. God will not tolerate disobedience in the life of the believer.

However, God is long-suffering and He will deal with the disobedience of the believer in a loving way because He is a God of unlimited mercy. God does not ask much of the believer. His laws and statutes are never overbearing to us. In fact, the scriptures teach us that His burden is light.

God will always carry the burden of the believer if the believer gives his burden to the Lord and leaves it there.

All of God's children are blessed through the promises that God made with Abraham. The believer is the seed of Abraham and heir to the promise. The covenant that God swore to Abraham belongs to every child of God and He is indeed a covenant keeper.

The scripture teaches us in **Deuteronomy 7:9**; *"Therefore know that the Lord your God, He is God, the faithful God Who keeps covenant and mercy for a thousand generations with those who love Him and keep His commandments."*

GOD'S PROMISES

In my study of God's word, I have noticed that God favors His children who obey Him and keep His commandments. He blesses His children with good health, but for the sinners, He places diseases on them and their families.

In **Exodus 15:26** the word of God tells us:

"If you diligently heed the voice of the Lord your God and do what is right in His sight, give ear to His commandments and keep all His statutes, I will put none of the diseases on you which I have brought on the Egyptians. For I am the Lord Who heals you."

Every believer should know that God can heal any disease. He wants to heal His children of all diseases. This is His word. We as God's children must be mindful of the goodness and mercy of our loving Father Who cares for us.

All believers should have a desire to succeed and prosper in life. It is in every human being to succeed at something in life. This does not mean that every person will succeed. In fact, many will not succeed for one reason or another. However, it is God Who causes the harvest to grow and yield its fruit, not people.

In **1 Kings 2:3** it says, *"And keep the charge of the Lord your God: to walk in His ways, to keep His statutes, His commandments, His judgments, and His testimonies, as it is written in the law of Moses, that you may prosper in all that you do and wherever you turn."*

I believe that longevity is linked to the obedience of God's commands and His statutes and that He gives long life to those believers who honor their parents.

It is written in **Ephesians 6:2-3;** *"Honor your father and mother, which is the first commandment with promise; that it may be well with you and you may live long on the earth."*

The Promise of a New Life

God will teach the believer obedience through suffering, for this is God's way of training. He taught Jesus obedience through suffering.

"Though He was a Son, yet He learned obedience by the things He suffered." **(Hebrews 5:8)**

God promises to show mercy (kindness) to the believer. *"But showing mercy (kindness) to thousands, to those who love Me and keep My commandments."* **(Deuteronomy 5:10)**

A Promise Of An Abundant Life To The Believer

The abundant life that is spoken of in **John 10:10** does not necessarily mean to have an abundance of material things in the life of the believer. However, a better definition of the abundant life that Jesus was referring to is the position of the believer when he has entered the kingdom of God and is enjoying all the benefits of the kingdom that includes all the promises of God and the fullness of life. This is the abundant life.

God delights in giving His children all things. The bible teaches us in **Psalm 35:27b;** *"God has pleasure in the prosperity of His servant."*

God wants to bless His children because He is the Potter, and his children are the clay. The believer who is living in righteousness is the trophy of God and it pleases God to be called their Father.

God knows how to give His children the things in life that are good for them. God will not give His children anything that will prove not to be good for them in the future.

GOD'S PROMISES

JESUS' PROMISE TO CONFESS THE BELIEVER'S NAME TO GOD

The bible teaches us that Jesus is our advocate and He is continually pleading our case before God.

The believer should always confess Jesus before the world to lift Him up. The bible teaches that if Jesus be lifted up, He would draw all men unto Him. When we confess the name of Jesus to others, He in turn confesses the believers name to God.

In the book of Matthew it tells us; *"Therefore whoever confesses Me before men, him I will confess before My Father Who is in heaven."* **(Matthew 10:32)**

Conversely, *"But whoever denies Me before men, him I will also deny before My Father Who is in heaven."* **(Matthew 10:33)**

THE BELIEVER WILL BECOME A NEW CREATION

The scripture teaches us in **2 Corinthians 5:17(NIV)**; *"Therefore, if anyone is in Christ, he is a new creation; the old has gone, the new has come."*

The believer shall be taught that the truth of life is in Jesus.

It is written:

"That you put off, concerning your former conduct, the old man which grows corrupt according to the deceitful lusts, and be renewed in the spirit of your mind, and that you put on the new man which was created according to God, in true righteousness and holiness." **(Ephesians 4:22-24)**

The bible teaches us that the new man shall set his mind on things above, not on things of the earth.

The Promise of a New Life

The new man must put to death the following: fornication, uncleanness, passion, evil desires, and covetousness, which is idolatry. Because of these things, the wrath of God is coming to the sons of disobedience.

The new man must put away the following: anger, wrath, malice, blasphemy, and filthy language out of your mouth.

Once the believer has put on the new man, he is renewed in knowledge according to the image of Him Who created him.

This new image of the believer is further confirmed when we consider that God made us in His image.

"Then God said, let Us make man in Our image, according to Our likeness; let them have dominion over the fish of the sea, over the birds of the air, and over the cattle, over all the earth and over every creeping thing that creeps on the earth." **(Genesis 1:26)**

Romans 6:4 teaches us that the baptism of the new believer symbolizes that he was baptized into Christ Jesus and also at the same time, his old flesh was spiritually baptized into death. *"Therefore we were buried with Him through baptism into death, that just as Christ was raised from the dead by the glory of the Father, even so we also should walk in newness of life."*

Therefore, the believer shall no longer be a slave to sin. The old man was crucified with Christ and we believe that we will also live with Him.

Chapter Six:

The Power of God's Word

GOD'S PROMISES

A PROMISE TO KNOW THE TRUTH THROUGH THE HOLY SPIRIT

Today, the believer may have to contend with the many doctrines heard. The believer must know what truth is and what error is. The scripture teaches us in **Revelation 12:9**; *"That ancient serpent called the devil or Satan deceives the whole world."* The believer must test all spirits with the word of God to make sure that he is hearing the truth. The bible tells us that many false prophets have gone out in the world to deceive the believer. God wants the believer to study to "show himself approved" to be able to rightly divide His word. God wants His children to know the truth. This is why He has given us His word and the Holy Spirit.

In **John 16:13** the scripture tells us; *"However, when He the Spirit of truth has come, He will guide you into all truth; for He will not speak on His own authority, but whatever He hears He will speak; and He will tell you of things to come."*

A PROMISE OF GOD TO FIGHT FOR THE BELIEVER

God wants the believer to live a life of peace with everyone and not respond in a way that will promote an argument. However, there will be times when the believer will be placed in situations where his only choice is to defend himself with the word of God.

It is always best to avoid a fight by calling on the Father for help. The word of God tells us that God will make a way for the believer to escape without harm. In any situation, God does not want the believer to avenge himself; because it is God Who will always avenge the believer.

The scripture teaches us that; *"The Lord shall fight for you, and you shall hold your peace."* **(Exodus 14:14)**

The Power of God's Word

JESUS PROMISED TO DO WHAT THE BELIEVER ASKS

All believers have needs and desires throughout life. He has needs for himself and needs for his loved ones. The bible teaches us that God wants to give the believer the desires of his heart. He also promises that He will supply all the needs of the believer according to His riches in glory by Christ Jesus. God wants to give His children good things. However, the things that God will give His children must be in His will.

The scripture teaches us in **John 14:13-14** how to ask for what we want:

"And whatever you ask in My name, that I will do, that the Father may be glorified in the Son." If you ask anything in My name, I will do it."

A True Story: Baby Karen was Born Unable to Breathe

On October 30th about 2 a.m., when Bill's daughter Karen was born, she was yellowish in color and not breathing. Bill's wife Anna said it seemed as though you could have heard a pin drop in the delivery room because the baby was not crying. Immediately they whisked the baby over to a table without even letting Anna hold her and began working to make her breathe. The doctors and nurses were rushing around in the delivery room in a sort of panic mode.

Bill and Anna are strong believers in God. Bill was somewhat unsure of what to do because everything was happening so fast. Anna told Bill to go and call their pastor to have him stand in agreement with them for little Karen's life. Anna said to God, "Lord, I know You did not give us this baby to take her right back from us." While Bill was making his way downstairs to call their pastor, Anna trusted God and did not doubt for one second that the baby was going to be alright.

Bill dialed the pastor's number and the phone must have rung ten or more times. It was about 2:30 a.m. Surely the pastor was asleep. Bill allowed the phone to continue to ring. Finally, the pastor answered the phone. Bill explained the situation to the pastor who was obviously somewhat drowsy from being awakened from sleep. The pastor began to pray and ask God for divine intervention.

After the pastor prayed, Bill headed back upstairs toward the delivery room. Before he had reached the final step to enter the hallway that the delivery room was on, he heard the baby crying loudly and thanked God for hearing and answering their prayer.

In the meantime, the doctor said they needed to run various tests on the baby because of the delayed time of her not breathing during the birth and delivery process that caused her to not get oxygen to her brain. He went on to state that as a result, she may not be normal.

Once again, Bill and Anna trusted God and did not agree with or receive anything negative concerning little Karen's health. The tests revealed what they already knew. Little Karen was fine and normal in every area.

―――――――――――――――――――

This situation reminds me that God never slumbers nor sleeps. In **Psalm 121:4,** the bible teaches us; *"Behold He who keeps Israel shall neither slumber nor sleep."*

A True Story: God Held Back the Rain

Linda picked her girls up from school every day because she did not want them to ride the bus. Kristy was in pre-K and Lisa was in kindergarten. On one particular day, as Linda was leaving home she noticed how cloudy it was. The sky was gray with thick, dark clouds and looked as if it could start raining at any moment. Linda prayed and asked God to, "Please hold back the rain," because the window on the driver side had recently quit working. It was a power window and was all the way down. The motor had gone out and the window could not be raised. She would have gotten soaked.

After picking the girls up from school, Linda proceeded on her way back home still praying and praising God for holding the rain back. She said; "God, You are awesome!" Kristy and Lisa jumped up and down laughing and said yeah! This was also an opportunity for them to witness the power of prayer and trusting God.

God Has Promised To Rescue The Believer Who Acknowledges His Name

In every believer's life, there will come a time when he will face trouble and will find the need to call upon the name of the Lord for help. The scripture teaches us that whoever calls upon the name of the Lord will be saved. Jesus has promised to protect the believer who calls upon him. He has also promised to give the believer a long life because he has loved the Lord.

The book of **Psalm 91:14-16 (NIV)** tells us, *"Because he loves Me, says the Lord, I will rescue him; I will protect him for he acknowledges My name. He will call upon Me and I will answer him; I will be with him in trouble, I will deliver him and honor him. With long life I will satisfy him and show him My salvation."*

GOD'S PROMISES

THE BELIEVER IS PROMISED THAT HE WILL BE TOGETHER WITH JESUS IN HEAVEN

Every believer knows that one day his natural life will end and he will live in the next life with Jesus throughout eternity. He believes that Jesus will return to get him and take him to live in heaven his eternal home.

It will be like a homecoming for all believers alike who have been given the gift of salvation. There will be no more sickness, no suffering, no crying and no dying. It is the place where the spirits of all believers long for once giving their life to Christ. The believer will be living the promise that Jesus made to all believers that He would one day come and receive them to Himself forever.

The scripture confirms this promise in the Book of John:

"In My Father's house there are many mansions, if it were not so I would have told you. I go to prepare a place for you. And if I go and prepare a place for you, I will come again and receive you to Myself; that where I am there you will be also." **(John 14:2-3)**

Chapter Seven:

God's Promise to Care for His Children

GOD'S PROMISES

GOD'S PROVIDENTIAL PROMISES

God the Father is a provider. He has promised to provide His children with all of their needs and desires.

We must believe and have faith that God will always do what His word says. God even provides for the animals and creatures on this planet. However, the believer is far more valuable than the animals.

The believer is a child of God and He has promised to care for them in a loving way.

Philippians 4:19 tells us; *"And My God shall supply all your needs according to His riches in glory by Christ Jesus."*

This is a promise that God has made to His people and He will always keep His promise.

It may appear, at times, that God will not show up in a situation where needed. Nevertheless, God will always come to our aid when He knows that it is time. He may not come when we want Him to, but He will come.

God does not want His children to be in a *'want'* position, so He made a promise to His people through a prayer taught in **Psalm 23:1-6:**

¹The Lord is my shepherd; I shall not want.

²He makes me to lie down in green pastures;

He leads me beside the still waters.

³He restores my soul; He leads me in the paths of righteousness For His name's sake.

⁴Yea, though I walk through the valley of the shadow of death, I will fear no evil; For You are with me; Your rod and Your staff, they comfort me.

God's Promise to Care for His Children

⁵You prepare a table before me in the presence of my enemies; You anoint my head with oil; My cup runs over.

⁶Surely goodness and mercy shall follow me all the days of my life; And I will dwell in the house of the Lord forever.

God will always take care of His own in a way that pleases Him. For His ways are always better than our ways. God knows everything that we need and He will always give the believer what is best for him. We do not always know what is best for us, but God does. He will give us what He knows is best at all times.

The scripture reminds us in **Psalm 34:8-9:** *"⁸Oh, taste and see that the Lord is good; Blessed is the man who trusts in Him! ⁹Oh, fear the Lord, you His saints! There is no want to those who fear Him."*

A PROMISE TO HEAL THE BELIEVER'S BODY

God has given the believer the promise to heal all his illnesses. We as believers do not have to live with any disease. Jesus received many stripes so that we could always be healed from any ailments.

In **Isaiah 53:5,** it says; *"But He was wounded for our transgressions, He was bruised for our iniquities; the chastisement for our peace was upon Him, and by His stripes we are healed."*

In the book of Psalm, scripture teaches us that God will always keep His word and heal our diseases. *"Bless the Lord, O my soul, and forget not all His benefits; Who forgives all your iniquities, Who heals all your diseases, Who redeems your life from destruction, Who crowns you with loving kindness and tender mercies."* **(Psalm 103:2-4)**

GOD'S PROMISES

It is written:

"Then your light shall break forth like the morning, Your healing shall spring forth speedily, and your righteousness shall go before you; The glory of the Lord shall be your rear guard." **(Isaiah 58:8)**

It is God's desire that His children be healed. God can heal the believer by sending His word. The believer can ask God for healing and God will send His word to heal.

In **Psalm 107:20,** the scripture speaks this truth in *"He sent His word and healed them, and delivered them from their destructions."*

Jesus told His disciples that He was going away and was not going to leave them without sending a Comforter to them. He also told His disciples that the things they saw Him do; they would do also, and greater things they would do, because He was going to the Father.

This is a promise from God that the believer of today who has the proper faith, will be able to do the same things that Jesus did when He was here on the earth.

The bible teaches us that Jesus went about the land healing the sick of all types of diseases.

In Matthew it tells us; *"Then His (Jesus') fame went throughout Syria, and they brought to Him all sick people, who were afflicted with various diseases and torments, and those who were demon possessed, epileptics, and paralytics; and He healed them."* **(Matthew 4:24)**

Many times Jesus did healing when He was not with the person who needed the healing. Jesus just spoke the word and healing would take place in the person's body.

There was a man in Capernaum who had a sick servant in his army and he asked Jesus to heal him. Jesus replied that He would go with the centurion to heal his servant. But the centurion replied — just say the word and he shall be healed.

In **Matthew 8:8,** *"The centurion answered and said; "Lord I am not worthy that You shall come under my roof. But only speak a word, and my servant will be healed."*

Jesus marveled at the centurion's faith and said that He had not seen such faith in Israel. He told the centurion to go on his way, and as he had believed, it would be done for him. The servant was healed in the same hour.

A True Story: A 50/50 Chance to Live after Surgery

Travis and his wife Beverly were watching television late on a Sunday night. Around 11:45 p.m., Travis turned to his wife Beverly and noticed that she was asleep. He gently shook her to wake her so she could go to bed. She did not respond so he tried again to wake her but to no avail. Travis called 911 and a medic was dispatched to their home. After checking Beverly, they rushed her to a nearby hospital. The doctor in the emergency examined her and ran several tests. He discovered that she was hemorrhaging in her brain. The doctor told Travis that his wife would need immediate surgery to stop the bleeding in her brain. He also said that there was a 50/50 chance that the surgery would be successful.

Travis asked the doctor could he be alone with his wife. The doctor agreed and left Beverly's room. Travis began to pray and cry out to God to heal his wife. He reminded God of His promise of **Isaiah 53:5;** *"By His stripes we are* *healed.*" Travis continued to pray while observing his wife who was asleep because of the medication she was given. After Travis finished praying for his wife, he told the doctor that he would return the next morning to check on his wife and he left.

The next morning Travis returned to the hospital and hurried to his wife's room. Beverly was sitting up in bed eating breakfast and smiling. She had no recollection of what had happened. She asked Travis why was she in the hospital. It appeared that Beverly's brain had completely erased about thirteen hours of her memory. Upon checking her, the doctor discovered that she was okay so he released her to go home.

Travis knew that God had healed his wife during the night. Today Beverly is doing fine with no after effects from the hemorrhaging in her brain.

THE LORD PROMISES TO HELP THE BELIEVER

When we commit our way to the Lord, He will direct our path. For He knows what is best for us. God knows how to make all things work out for the best for His children. There are no trial and error strategies in the kingdom of God. He wants His children to be successful in everything they do. When we trust in God, we cannot go wrong. He always has the best in mind for the believer.

God will see to it that the believer gets justice and proper treatment in every situation. God wants the believer to commit his life and everything he does to Him.

In **Psalm 37:5** it tells us; "*Commit your way to the Lord, trust also in Him, and He shall bring it to pass.*"

God's Promise to Care for His Children

We must always remember that God wants to help us in every aspect of our life. He wants to be the Father of all of our deeds and ambitions.

The scripture teaches us in **Proverbs 3:5-6:** *"Trust in the Lord with all your heart, and lean not on your own understanding; In all your ways acknowledge Him, and He shall direct your paths."*

"Fear not, for I am with you; be not dismayed, for I am your God. I will strengthen you, yes, I will help you. I will uphold you with my righteous right hand." **(Isaiah 41:10)**

In the book of **Psalm 71:12-13A,** it tells us that God is never far from His children. *"O God, do not be far from me; O my God, make haste to help me! Let them be confounded and consumed who are adversaries of my life."*

The believer must always remember that God will always help him, if he only trusts and have faith.

The scripture teaches us in Psalm; *"O Israel, trust in the Lord; He is their help and their shield. O house of Aaron, trust in the Lord; He is their help and their shield. You who fear the Lord, trust in the Lord; He is their help and their shield."* **(Psalm 115:9-11)**

The believer is required to use faith to please God for He responds to faith. The believer must also learn this truth; that faith is the only way to please Him.

The scripture teaches us in **Hebrews 11:6;** *"But without faith it is impossible to please Him, for he who comes to God must believe that He is, and that He is a rewarder of those who diligently seek Him."*

God has His children on His mind because He is a God of Love. He is a Father of the believer and He wants to give the believer all things that are good for Him. This promise can be found in **Romans 8:32;** *"He Who did not spare His own son, but delivered Him up for us all, how shall He not with Him also freely give us all things?"*

All believers who are serving the Lord will receive a reward that is promised by God. God will always honor His promises to His children. He desires to make all of His promises available to His own.

The scripture teaches us in **2 Corinthians 1:20;** *"For all the promises of God in Him (Jesus) are Yes, and in Him Amen, to the glory of God through us."*

In whatever you do, do it heartily as to the Lord, and not to men. It is God, who will honor your good deeds. He will see to it that the believer will be compensated.

The bible teaches us in **Colossians 3:24;** *"Knowing that from the Lord you will receive the reward of the inheritance; for you serve the Lord Christ."*

God will always send help to His children who are depending on Him. The believer who calls on the name of the Lord will be saved.

In **Psalm 33:20-21** it tells us; *"Our soul waits for the Lord; He is our help and our shield. For our heart shall rejoice in Him, because we have trusted in His holy Name."*

God has promised to be our helper and protector and His word tells us in **Psalm 41:1;** *"Blessed is the one who considers the poor; the Lord will deliver (help) him in time of trouble."*

The bible teaches us that there will always be trouble in the world. Jesus teaches that in Him there is peace; and to be of good cheer, for He has overcome the world and its trouble. Since Jesus has overcome the world and He lives on the inside of us, we can also overcome the world.

My True Story: Caught in the Snow without Snow Tires

One afternoon around 4 p.m., I was driving north on interstate 85 leaving Atlanta, GA heading toward Spartanburg, SC. I had the radio on and heard the announcer give a weather report about the possibility of snow in the Clemson, SC area. I had to go through Clemson to get to my destination. In approximately one hour as I was driving north, snowflakes began to cover my windshield. Gradually the falling snow increased to the point that my windshield wipers could barely remove the snow from my view. I had to use my left hand to reach outside the car to help the wiper blade operate. Finally, the traffic in front of me came to a stop. I was in a traffic jam. It was about 7:30 p.m., and because of the heavy snowfall, it was dark. As I looked ahead of me, I could see cars lined up for ten or fifteen miles or more. I checked my gas supply and it was okay. I was sitting in my car wondering when the traffic was going to move. The driver of the car ahead of me got out of his car, opened his trunk and pulled out a six-pack of beer. He must have anticipated being stuck in traffic for a while.

After sitting there in traffic for over an hour, I heard a voice in my spirit tell me to go around the traffic. I did not think this was a good idea because I did not have snow tires on my car. But, the voice said it again, "go around the cars that are in front of you." If I went around the cars, this would mean I would be on the median, which had grass beneath the snow. I obeyed the voice and proceeded to go around the cars that were stopped in front of me. As I drove on the median, my back tires began to spin and the back end of the car began to sway to the left and to the right. I called out to Jesus for help. I said; "Jesus, Jesus help me!" Each time I said Jesus the back tires would stop spinning and I would get traction and continue to move ahead. When I stopped saying "Jesus help me," the back tires would start to spin again. So I would say Jesus, Jesus help me and the tires would stop spinning. As I drove on the median passing the cars stopped on my right side, the drivers would look at me with a look of astonishment. They probably thought that what I was doing was too much of a risk to take. I must have passed a thousand cars or more.

Finally, I came to the lead vehicle of the traffic jam. It was a semi truck without the trailer attached blocking the lanes. The driver had abandoned his truck and walked away. God knew this, and that was why He placed the thought in my mind to go around all those vehicles in the first place. I drove on to my destination without any problems.

———

I learned at an early age that I can do all things through Christ when I ask Him for help. He has never failed me; no not one time. He promised never to leave me.

There will certainly come a time when every believer will require the help of God. It may happen during normal situations and circumstances of life or it may be a troubling event. Regardless, God always promises to be an "ever present" help. We must simply call on Him.

Psalm 46:1 tells us; *"God is our refuge and strength, a very present help in trouble."*

In **Psalm 124:8,** we learn: *"Our help is in the name of the Lord, Who made heaven and earth."*

God knows the right time to give His servant strength and power. He will wait for you to call for help.

There will be times in the life of the believer when he will become depressed or saddened in his spirit. His countenance may even show his grief. However, when God sees His child in this condition, He is always available to come to his aid.

"Why are you cast down, O my soul? And why are you disquieted (depressed) within me? Hope in God; For I shall yet praise Him, the help of my countenance and my God." (**Psalm 42:11**)

God's Promise to Care for His Children

"Our soul waits for the Lord; He is our help and shield. For our heart shall rejoice in Him, because we have trusted in His holy name. Let Your mercy, O Lord, be upon us, just as we hope in You." **(Psalm 33:20-22)**

A Prayer of Thanks for the Promise to Help

Oh God,

Do not be far from me, Oh my God. Make haste to help me. For You are my shield and defense in time of trouble. I have kept Your name in my heart for peace and tranquility. My soul knows Your Spirit that dwells inside of me. You are always there in time of need. Your word is pure; and You are a shield to everyone who puts their trust in You. I thank You for the promise to help in time of need, in Jesus' Name.

Amen.

A True Story: She Cried Out To God To Save Her

Brenda was driving east on I-20 headed downtown Atlanta when a mattress fell off the truck in front of her car. There was not enough time to avoid hitting the mattress. The mattress was tangled up beneath Brenda's car. It wrapped itself around the drive shaft of her car. Her car went out of control and turned around in the street several times. Brenda cried out to God, "help me Father, save me Jesus and bring this car under control." God answered her prayer. The car stopped spinning and came to a stop on the side of the road. God saved her from having a serious accident and spared Brenda's life.

GOD'S PROMISES

"He shall call upon Me and I will answer him; I will be with him in trouble; I will deliver him and honor him." **(Psalm 91:15)**

A Promise Of Good Health For The Believer

The bible teaches us that good health for God's children is truly one of the blessings of God. As the scripture teaches that God provides strength and power to His children, this is also a clear indication that He desires good health for His children.

The scripture teaches us in **Proverbs 3:7-8;** *"Do not be wise in your own eyes; fear the Lord and depart from evil. It will be health to your flesh, and strength to your bones."*

God has seen to it that the believer will always have good health. He has promised us health in His word. The believer must only believe and stand on the promise of God.

"But He was wounded for our transgressions, He was bruised for our iniquities; the chastisement for our peace was upon Him, and by His stripes we are healed." **(Isaiah 53:5)**

The bible teaches us that God wants to bless His children with so much. However, He wants the believer to obey His word and delight himself in the things of God, for God desires to be glorified, honored, obeyed and praised by His children. The believer must hide the word of God in his heart, and meditate on it day and night. He should be careful and never allow the word of God to grow cold in his life.

"My son, give attention to my words; incline your ear to my sayings. Do not let them depart from your eyes; keep them in the midst of your heart; For they are life to those who find them, and health to all their flesh." **(Proverbs 4:20-22)**

God's Promise to Care for His Children

The believer should guard his words and choose them carefully. A believer can speak blessings or a curse on his own body. This is the power of the word of God and the believer should never say anything that he does not want to live with. In **Proverbs 18:21** it tells us; *"Death and life is in the power of the tongue, and those who love it will eat its fruit."*

The believer should choose his words when he speaks to others because even idle words can be harmful in a psychological way. When the believer speaks to others, his words should be to help others, bless others or to uplift others.

The bible tells us in **Proverbs 16:24;** *"Pleasant words are like a honeycomb, sweetness to the soul, and health to the bones."*

In **3 John 1,** Paul writes a letter to Gaius, the Elder, *"Beloved, I pray that you may prosper in all things and be in health, just as your soul prospers."*

A Prayer of Thanks for The Promise of Health

Father,

You have so patiently provided good health to my body for many years. You have provided good health since my day of conception in my mother's womb. I glorify Your name and give You all the honor and praise in Your precious Son's name, and I thank You for this precious promise of health.

In Jesus name,

Amen.

GOD'S PROMISES

A Promise Of Rest For The Believer

All believers will face, at times, burdens that seem to be overbearing and burdensome. Rest is one of the benefits that God gives to the believer who has entered the Kingdom of God. The Kingdom of God is on the inside of every committed believer. After a person has received Jesus Christ as his Savior, God's rest is available to that person. This is the place that God wants every believer to be once he has received salvation. In God's rest is where you will find all of the Promises of God. God's rest is the place where struggles of the believer end. It is the place where God is the ultimate provider of all your needs and desires.

"Come to me, all you who labor and are heavy laden, and I will give you rest." **(Matthew 11:28)**

A Promise Of Protection To The Believer

The bible teaches us that there will always be trouble in the world. For it is written: *"These things I have spoken to you, that in me you may have peace. In the world you will have tribulation; but be of good cheer, for I have overcome the world."* **(John 16:33)**

God desires to protect us, just as a shepherd protects his sheep. He is concerned about every one of them. If one of the sheep is missing, the shepherd will proceed to find the lost sheep.

The bible teaches that God will protect His children in time of trouble. He said that He would deliver them from their troubles.

In **Psalm 41:1** it says; *"Blessed is he who considers the poor; the Lord will deliver him in time of trouble."*

God's Promise to Care for His Children

A believer will face so many things in life. Many of them will be out of the control of the believer's power to do anything. There may be times when a believer is traveling in an automobile when another driver may be driving in the wrong lane and a potential accident could happen. However, God's divine intervention takes over to protect the believer who trusts in His Savior.

The believer could be traveling on an airplane when the engine of the plane malfunctions. This could cause the plane to lose altitude and crash. The believer who is committed to God can call on Jesus in times of trouble and He will answer. He can call on God's ministering angels to land the plane safely or to prevent the plane from having a crash.

I do believe that there are times when God will shield the believer from being injured because the blessing of God is on the believer. God will always protect and help His own. This is one of His promises for the believer to live by, and to expect.

The bible teaches in **Proverbs 30:5a;** *"Every word of God is pure. He is a shield to those who put their trust in Him."*

God desires to watch over the believer and direct his path, which ensures him of his safety and well-being. We as believers do not always know when or where there is danger.

Nothing is hidden from God. He is omnipresent and knows everything, which includes all potential danger that is lurking in various places in the earth. It is always wise to ask God for directions.

God will protect the believer from all danger when the believer is depending on God for safety.

The scripture teaches us that we can ask God for help on a daily basis for protection and direction.

GOD'S PROMISES

Proverbs 3:5-6 tells us; *"Trust in the Lord with all your heart, and lean not on your own understanding; In all your ways acknowledge Him and He shall direct your paths."*

When the believer asks God to direct his path, God will do just that. He will lead the believer to his destination safely and without danger. Because God will always honor the believer's request, it is wise to acknowledge God before an automobile trip, airplane trip or any type of trip because there is nothing that God cannot control.

It is also good to ask God to direct your path before you enter a meeting or session. God wants to guide you in all your ways. The believer can never know what may happen in any environment he finds himself in.

God's protection is always the best, and the wise believer should always ask God for directions.

The believer can always look to God for help. This is a promise from the Lord that He will never sleep nor slumber, and He will always be there to aid the believer. The believer must remember to call on God.

The scripture teaches us in the book of Psalm; *"I will lift up my eyes to the hills from whence comes my help? My help comes from the Lord, Who made heaven and earth."* **(Psalm 121:1-2)**

═══════════════════════

God is always near to the believer and He can be a shield for him. He has made promises to the believer to protect him.

In **Psalm 3:3-6** it says; *"But you, O Lord, are a shield for me, my glory and the One Who lifts up my head. I cried to the Lord with my voice, and He heard me from His holy hill. I lay down and slept; I awoke for the Lord sustained me. I will not be afraid of ten thousands of people, who have set themselves against me all around."*

God's Promise to Care for His Children

A Prayer of Thanks for the Promise of Protection

Father,

I know that You are with me, and You will protect me wherever I may go. You are my shield and my strength.

I will give You praise for I know that I am safe in Your Presence. You will always be with me wherever I go. In Jesus name,

Amen.

God's Promises Are His Word

The scripture teaches us that all of God's promises are yes, and they are binding. The believer can be assured that God's promises are His word and therefore, we can rely on them. When God makes a promise, there is no greater one that He can swear to but Himself, so He swore to Himself.

In **2 Corinthians 1:20** the scripture teaches us: *"For all the promises of God in Him are Yes, and in Him Amen, to the glory of God through us."*

The promises of God are something that we can always count on because it is God's word. We as believers should never doubt God's word.

When we look at this vast universe and observe the awesome power of God that has been manifested in our planetary system, how can we not trust God?

This same power raised Jesus from the dead and the same power supports every promise that God has made to us. God is our Father and it pleases Him to call us His children.

Chapter Eight:

The Eternal Promises

GOD'S PROMISES

GOD'S ETERNAL BLESSINGS TO THE BELIEVER

The scripture teaches us that the believer will live out two lives; the natural life and the spiritual life. The believer's natural life will end at his death. However, at the end of the natural life, the spiritual life begins. This life will last forever for the believer and it is referred to as eternal life.

In **1 John 2:17** this scripture tells us; *"The world and its desires pass away, but the man who does the will of God lives forever."*

This indeed is a promise from God to live forever with Him. The believer who fears God and keeps His commandments is doing the will of God and his reward is eternal life!

A PROMISE OF ETERNAL LIFE

The scriptures teach us that those who believe in Jesus will inherit eternal life.

"For God so loved the world that He gave His only begotten Son, that whoever believes in Him should not perish, but have everlasting life." **(John 3:16)**

God has made eternal life available for all people. It is not God's desire that any shall perish. However, many people will not choose to believe in the Son of God for salvation. Many will be deceived by the devil. The scripture teaches us that the devil has deceived the whole world!

"So the great dragon was cast out, that serpent of old, called the Devil and Satan, who deceives the whole world; he was cast to the earth, and his angels were cast out with him." **(Revelation 12:9)**

The Eternal Promises

This is a direct promise from God, that all who believe in Jesus will have eternal life, and all who do not believe shall perish. Those who have fully decided not to believe in Jesus Christ for whatever reason have rejected Him.

We all have a sin debt that must be paid. This is the reason that God sent His only begotten Son to this earth to die for man's sin. God did not want man to be condemned to die for his own sin. The death of Jesus is the only hope for man to escape the penalty of death. God promised salvation to anyone who would repent of his sins and accept Jesus as his Savior.

"The Lord is not slack concerning His promise, as some count slackness, but is longsuffering toward us, not willing that any should perish but that all should come to repentance." **(2 Peter 3:9)**

The scripture teaches that Jesus is the only way to eternal life, and no one can get to the Father in heaven except through Him.

Jesus came to the world to save sinners from their sin by shedding His blood on the cross and dying for them. As the penalty for sin is death, Jesus was the substitute for our death. Therefore, the believer does not have to pay for his sin debt because Jesus paid the sin debt for all who receive Him as their Savior.

Eternal life is a gift from God to all people through His Son Jesus Christ.

No one can work for salvation because it is a gift from God. It cannot be earned or purchased.

The bible teaches us:

"For by grace you have been saved through faith, and that not of yourselves; it is a gift of God, not of works lest anyone should boast." **(Ephesians 2:8-9)**

Once a person has received Jesus into his life as Savior and Lord, he is a fellow citizen with other saints and a member of the household of God. He now has the right to approach the throne of the Almighty God at anytime for help or any requests that he may have in life.

God desires that His children shall have the dreams of their hearts, for God Himself has placed many dreams in the hearts of His children. All dreams and desires are contained in the promises of God.

The bible teaches us in Romans; *"God Who did not spare His own Son, but gave Him up for us all, how shall He not with Him also freely give us all things?"* **(Romans 8:32)**

God knows that we all have needs and He cares for us, therefore, He will provide for us. We must commit ourselves to Him and believe His word.

The bible teaches us in **Matthew 6:33;** *"But seek first the kingdom of God and His righteousness, and all these things shall be added to you."*

Eternal life is a promise that all believers look forward to receiving. This promise gives hope to the believer and should give him a life of expectancy. It is a joy to know that we will live in heaven with Jesus forever and ever!

Eternal life is not for sale. It is a gift from God; given to every person who repents of his sins, believes that Jesus died for their sins, and God raised Him from the dead. The next step is to invite Jesus to come into their life as Savior and Lord.

In the book of **Romans 6:23** it tells us; *"For the wages of sin is death, but the gift of God is eternal life in Christ Jesus our Lord."*

The Eternal Promises

A Prayer of Thanks for Eternal Life

Heavenly Father,

My heart is full of joy as I think of my life knowing that I will live with You in heaven one day. You have blessed me with a wonderful promise of eternal life that gives my soul peace and tranquility, which surpasses all human understanding. I will always praise You in the name of Jesus, my Savior forever, and I will glorify Your name to others! I thank You for the promise of eternal life.

Amen.

A Promise Of Rapture

The scripture teaches us that Jesus will return to receive the believers and take them with Him to heaven. This is a promise from God Himself. This teaching can be found in 1 Thessalonians 4:16-18.

"For the Lord Himself will descend from heaven with a shout, with the voice of an archangel, and with the trumpet of God, and the dead in Christ will rise first. Then we who are alive and remain shall be caught up together with them in the clouds to meet the Lord in the air. And thus, we shall always be with the Lord. Therefore comfort one another with these words."

The believers that are alive when Christ returns will be caught up in the clouds to meet with those who are dead. This implies that there are believers who will not experience an earthly death. However, their earthly bodies will be transformed into a body like Jesus, which is a heavenly body. No flesh can enter heaven.

Remember the incorruptible and the corruptible. No corruptible body can enter heaven. The dead in Christ will rise first. Then the believers who are alive and remain will be caught up second.

Christ will return with the believers who are already with him whose bodies are in the grave. Remember when a believer dies, his spirit goes to be with the Lord in the blink of an eye. Their spirits will rest with the Lord until the rapture and they will return with the Lord to receive those who are waiting for the rapture.

The bible teaches us that not all believers shall sleep (die). This can be found in **1 Corinthians 15:51-57**. *"Behold, I tell you a mystery: 'We shall not all sleep, but we shall all be changed—in a moment, in the twinkling of an eye, at the last trumpet. For the trumpet will sound, and the dead will be raised incorruptible, and we shall be changed. For this corruptible must put on incorruption, and this mortal must put on immortality. So when this corruptible has put on incorruption, and this mortal has put on immortality, then shall be brought to pass the saying that is written: 'Death is swallowed up in victory.' 'O Death, where is your sting? O Hades, where is your victory?'*

The sting of death is sin, and the strength of sin is the law. But thanks be to God, Who gives us the victory through our Lord Jesus Christ."

A PROMISE TO PREPARE A PLACE IN HEAVEN

Jesus told His disciples that He would leave them and go to His Father in heaven. In His Father's house there are many mansions and He would prepare a place for them. At the appointed time, He would return to receive them.

Jesus said to the disciples that He is the way, the truth and the life. He also stated that no one could come to the Father except through Him. In other words, Jesus is the only 'Way' to eternal life and salvation. God is the only One Who can draw a person to Jesus. No one can decide to be saved on his own accord.

But as it is written:

"Eye has not seen, nor ear heard, Nor have entered into the heart of man The things which God has prepared for Those who love Him." **(1 Corinthians 2:9)**

"Let not your heart be troubled; you believe in God, believe also in Me. In My Father's house are many mansions; if it were not so, I would have told you. I go to prepare a place for you." **(John 14: 1-2)**

"But now they desire a better, that is, a heavenly country. Therefore God is not ashamed to be called their God, for He has prepared a city for them." **(Hebrews 11:1**

Chapter Nine:

The Children of God will be Glorified

GOD'S PROMISES

A Promise To Be Glorified With Jesus

The scripture teaches us that Jesus learned obedience through the things he suffered. If Christ suffered for the things he learned, then we as followers of Christ must also suffer with him. The bible teaches us that obedience is learned through suffering. God requires obedience from His children. God has placed Jesus as our example to follow.

God was glorified through the things that Jesus suffered and God will be glorified through the things that His children will suffer.

The scripture teaches us in **Romans 8:16-17;** *"The Spirit Himself bears witness with our spirit that we are children of God, and if children, then heirs— heirs of God and joint heirs with Christ, if indeed we suffer with him, that we may also be glorified together."*

The believer should count the suffering with Jesus as an honor, because it pleases God to give honor to His son and to His children.

God Promised To Be The Believer's Guide

The believer who depends on God for everything has learned to trust God. God wants to be everything to the believer. God is the Father and Maker of the believer and He knows the needs of His children. For He is the Potter and we are the clay. He will shape and mold us to have the character of His Son Jesus if we allow Him and never give up.

God wants us to depend totally on Him for all of our needs. He is our provider and comforter. The believer that looks to God for all his needs and concerns will be guided by Him.

The Children of God will be Glorified

We must give God thanks for all that He does for us regularly. Often times we take the blessings of God for granted and never stop to count our blessings. How quick we are as believers to forget that God is our guardian and He cares deeply for us. We complain when circumstances get uncomfortable. God has helped us in the past, and He will help us in the future. He promised never to forsake us.

We must remember His goodness and greatness. He will always care for us in wonderful ways.

God extends His love to us so that we may show love to others.

"For this is God, our God forever and ever; He will be our guide even to death." (**Psalm 48:14**)

For God is always guiding His children in a manner that keeps them in safety and away from harm; even when we are not aware of it.

"But the Lord is faithful Who will establish you and guard you from the evil one." (**2 Thessalonians 3:3**)

A PROMISE TO DO GREAT WORK

Jesus did much work on the earth; healing the sick, giving sight to the blind, raising the dead and cleansing the lepers. He did these things to glorify God the Father. One of His disciples asked Him who had sinned that the man was born blind. Jesus answered and said that no one had sinned that he was born blind, but this happened so that God would be glorified when the man received his sight.

When a believer does the work of God, God is glorified. The believer is to do the same work that Jesus did when He was on the earth.

The bible teaches us that the work Jesus did, the believer can do also because Jesus went to the Father. This means that the believer who has proper faith in Jesus, can do all the things that Jesus did such as heal the sick, raise the dead, give sight to the blind, cast out demons, teach His word with authority, perform miracles, etc. when doing it in His name. However, the body of Christ (believers, as a whole) can do greater things than Jesus did while he was on earth.

A Promise Of Faith

Without faith it is impossible to please God, so God has given each one of us a measure of faith. The scripture tells us in Romans; *"For I say, through the grace given to me, to everyone who is among you, not to think of himself more highly than he ought to think, but to think soberly, as God Who has dealt to each one a measure of faith."* **(Romans 12:3)**

It is up to the believer to grow in faith as his Father in heaven gives him his portion of faith, as he grows in the things of God, through Jesus. In the book of Hebrews it tells us; *"Now faith is the substance of things hoped for, the evidence of things not seen."* **(Hebrews 11:1)**

God will teach His children faith and trust, for it is faith that pleases Him. God will place His children in circumstances to develop their faith and trust in Him. This will lead to suffering and pain at times. We as believers should never consider this action from God as punishment because it is not. It is only teaching that will result in obedience and it is suffering that will lead to an improved character.

The Children of God will be Glorified

In **2 Timothy 4:7,** the bible teaches us; *"I have fought the good fight, I have finished the race, I have kept the faith."*

Psalm 34:17 tells us; *"The righteous cry out, and the Lord hears, and delivers them out of all their troubles."*

Remember that faith is the practice of believing in that which God says.

Chapter Ten:

God's Children Will Lead

GOD'S PROMISES

A Promise To Be A Leader

When the believer obeys the word of God and has made a commitment to follow Him, he has positioned himself to receive God's best. God will give the committed believer favor by making him a leader in whatever he is doing. Why, because God's word clearly says in the book of **Deuteronomy 28:13;** *"And the Lord shall make you the head and not the tail; you shall be above only and not beneath, if you heed the commandments of the Lord your God, which I command you today, and are careful to observe them."* God is always observing any believer who loves His commandments and this is one way to get God's attention.

The bible tells us that God is good to those who delight in His commandments. God gives favor to those who love Him and seek to know Him better. All things that the believer wants will be given if these things are in the will of God.

The scripture teaches us in the book of Matthew; *"But seek first the kingdom of God and His righteousness, and all these things shall be added to you."* **(Matthew 6:33)**

God has also promised the believer that he would be the head and not the tail. He would be prosperous going in and prosperous coming out. The Lord favors the believer who is trusting in Him and He gives him power to be the best in anything he set his mind to do.

The scripture teaches us that with God we can do all things and without Him we can do nothing. One of the key things to do as a believer is always abide in the word of God, and have the word of God abiding in you.

God wants to be first in the believer's life. Nothing in the believer's life should come before God. The believer can make God happy by committing his life to Him.

God's Children Will Lead

The bible tells us that God is glorified when the believer is prosperous in the things he is doing. God does not get any pleasure when the believer is not successful and is failing. All success will come to the believer when his ways are pleasing to God. This is the promise that God has made to all believers.

GOD'S PROMISE TO SUSTAIN THE BELIEVER

There is a tendency to give up sometimes when a trial comes our way. In other words, we want to move away from the appropriate way of responding to the trial and respond in our own way, not God's way. The word of God tells us that the Holy Spirit (our Comforter) will come to our aid to help us. We must remember that every trial sent by God is for our training so that we may be partakers of His holiness.

There will be times in the believer's life when burdens will become overbearing to him. Whatever situation we find ourselves in, Jesus says to bring all of our burdens to Him.

"Come to Me, all you who labor and are heavy laden, and I will give you rest. Take My yoke upon you and learn from Me. For I am gentle and lowly in heart, and you will find rest for your souls. For My yoke is easy and My burden is light." **(Matthew 11:28-30)**

God will always care for His children and will always watch over us because He loves us. God has promised to sustain us and protect us and will never allow us to be moved. This is His promise to all of His children.

The scripture teaches us; *"Cast your burden on the Lord, and He shall sustain you; He shall never permit the righteous to be moved."* **(Psalm 55:22)**

GOD'S PROMISES

GOD PROMISED TO SHOW YOU GREAT THINGS

How delightful would it be, if the believer could see great and mighty things of God? There are so many things that we do not know about God that are still a mystery to the mind of the believer. We know what the bible says about God and we know what is revealed to us through the Holy Spirit, yet there is so much more that the believer does not know about God. God tells us to go to His word with anticipation and trust in Him to wait for the answer to our prayers.

There are great and mighty things I would like to know about the Holy Spirit. There are great and mighty things I would like to know about the Kingdom of God and the kingdom of heaven. The bible teaches us that if we ask God about these great and mighty things and diligently seek Him, He will show us His secret things and His mighty things. There are so many mysteries in the bible and there are many mysteries in the working of God. One of the reasons for the mysteries is that God's ways are so much higher than ours.

The bible teaches us in the book of Isaiah: *"For My thoughts are not your thoughts, nor are your ways My ways," says the Lord. "For as the heavens are higher than the earth, so are My ways higher than your ways, and My thoughts than your thoughts."* **(Isaiah 55:8-9)**

"Call to Me, and I will answer you, and show you great and mighty things, which you do not know." **(Jeremiah 33:3)**

A PROMISE TO TAKE SICKNESS AWAY

The bible teaches us that God will remove sickness from those who serve Him. God says that he will bless the water the believer drinks and the food the believer eats. Therefore, there will be no sickness from water and there will be no sickness from food once God has blessed it. This is the power of God. He protects His children from any harm or danger in anything that the believer ingests. Nothing that God has blessed can harm the believer. God has given His word and His word will always prevail over any opposition.

God has made the believer, just as He has made bread, water, and everything else. The bible tells us in **John 1:3;** *"All things were made through Him, and without Him nothing was made that was made."*

Man cannot make anything with his own power, nor can man create anything on his own account. Man does have the power to corrupt what God has made because of the sin that has entered through Adam. For God is the Creator of all things, including the Devil himself.

The scripture teaches us; *"So you shall serve the Lord your God, and He will bless your bread, and your water, and I will take sickness away from the midst of you."* **(Exodus 23:25)**

THE PROMISE OF GOOD THINGS

The bible teaches us that God desires to give His children good things and He has pleasure in the prosperity of His saints. There is no good thing that God will withhold from those who love Him. However, God does require the believer to be obedient to His word and commandments. He has promised to be the believers helper at all times. God has made promises to believers who are good in His sight.

"For God gives wisdom and knowledge and joy to a man who is good in His sight; but to the sinner He gives the work of gathering and collecting, that he may give to him who is good before God." **(Ecclesiastes 2:26)**

Wisdom, knowledge, and joy are only a few benefits that are available to the believer who diligently seeks God. God wants the very best for His children. He will not settle for second best for His children. God says in His word that if an earthly father knows how to give gifts to his children, how much more will your Father Who is in heaven give good things to those who ask Him?

God's word tells us in the book of Psalm; *"The young lions lack and suffer hunger; but those who seek the Lord shall not lack any good thing."* **(Psalm 34:10)**

Finally, the believer's righteous relationship with God begins with seeking God! Seeking God is the 'pivoting point' of the entire New Testament.

The 'Kingdom of God' will open up to the believer who is totally committed to seeking God with everything that is in him

Chapter Eleven:

God Will Always Be With You

GOD'S PROMISES

THE PROMISE TO NEVER LEAVE OR FORSAKE YOU

There are times in scripture where God has promised that He will not leave or forsake His children. When a believer is committed to God, this promise will always be true. He will not forsake His children. God is like a parent to all His children and He would never leave any of His children who walk in His ways.

In **Deuteronomy 31:6** it says, *"Be strong and of good courage, do not fear nor be afraid of them; for the Lord your God, He is the one who goes with you. He will not leave you nor forsake you."*

The believer can always count on the Lord to be with him at all times. God's word tells us that He is always there by our side ready to tend to our needs.

God will never leave His children because He has made a vow never to leave them. God will always honor His word. We as believers must always trust Him and hold on to His promises that will always sustain us.

The scripture also teaches us that not even death can separate us from the love of God. For He so loved the world that He gave His only Son to die for the sins of the whole world. The love of God is indescribable and incomprehensible. We are greatly blessed with knowing that nothing on earth can separate us from the love of God.

God's word is His voice and when we read His word, we are actually hearing His voice. And as we hear His voice, we must always receive what we read as if God Himself is talking to us personally.

God says to every believer in the book of **ROMANS 8:38-39**; *"For I am persuaded that neither death nor life, nor angels nor principalities nor power, nor things present nor things to come, nor height nor depth, nor any other created thing, shall be able to separate us from the love of God which is in Christ Jesus our Lord."*

God Will Always Be With You

THE PROMISE TO HEAR YOUR PRAYERS

The scripture teaches us that; *"The Lord is far from the wicked, but He hears the prayer of the righteous."* **(Proverbs 15:29)**

There will come a time when every believer will need God to hear his prayer. Why? Because the bible teaches us in **John 16:33** that *"These things I have spoken to you, that in Me you may have peace. In the world you will have tribulation; but be of good cheer, I have overcome the world."*

"And the prayer of faith will save the sick, and the Lord will raise him up. And if he has committed sins, he will be forgiven." **(James 5:15)**

The bible teaches us that the Lord is our strength in time of trouble. The believer should always pray for strength for himself and others. When we pray for strength, the Lord will help the believer and deliver him.

There will be times in the believer's life when he will feel weakness and will not know how or what to ask in prayer.

However, the Holy Spirit is our helper. It is written, *"Likewise the Spirit also helps in our weaknesses. For we do not know what we should pray for as we ought, but the Spirit Himself makes intercession for us with groanings which cannot be uttered."* **(Romans 8:26)**

Jesus has said in the scriptures that the believer can pray for what he wants in His name, and He will do it, that the Father may be glorified in the Son. **(John 14:13)**

Jesus is the believer's intercessor, always interceding on behalf of the believer. He is also our High Priest, praying to God for the needs of the believer.

God told the people of Israel that if they would humble themselves and pray to Him, He would heal their land.

GOD'S PROMISES

God is always available to hear the prayers of His righteous servants. The believer can pray at any place and at anytime. God will answer his prayers.

Jeremiah 29:12: *"Then you will call upon Me and go and pray to Me, and I will listen to you. And you will seek Me and you will find Me, when you seek Me with all your heart."*

The scripture teaches us that; *"The effective, fervent prayer of a righteous man avails much."* **(James 5:16b)**

God wants to be the only source of all good things the believer needs and desires. We should ask God for what we want through our prayers to Him.

It is written in **Matthew 21:22:** *"And whatever things you ask in prayer, believing, you will receive."*

If we have faith when we pray, whatever we ask God for, He hears us; And if we know that He hears us, whatever we ask for will be ours if it is His will for us.

God responds to the faith of His children.

"Then you shall call, and the Lord will answer; You shall cry, and He will say, 'Here I am.' If you take away the yoke from your midst, the pointing of the finger, and speaking wickedness." **(Isaiah 58:9)**

In **Hebrews 11:6**, it teaches us; *"But without faith it is impossible to please Him, for He who comes to God must believe that He is, and that He is a rewarder of those who diligently seek Him."*

God's eyes and ears are always on His children to honor His promises to them and to care for their needs on a daily basis. He said He would never leave or forsake us. All believers can depend on God to keep His word.

The scripture teaches us in **1 Peter 3:12;** *"For the eyes of the Lord are on the righteous, and His ears are open to their prayers; but the face of the Lord is against those who do evil."*

"Now this is the confidence that we have in Him, that if we ask anything according to His will He hears us, and if we know that He hears us, whatever we ask, we know that we have the petitions that we have asked of Him." **(1 John 5:14-15)**

A True Story: I Petitioned God for Help to Sell a Property

It is written in **Philippians 4:6,** *"Be anxious for nothing, but through prayer, supplication and thanksgiving, let your request be known to God and the peace that surpasses all understanding will guard your hearts and minds through Christ Jesus."*

In the fall of 2005, I owned a strip plaza in Riverdale, Georgia. I had invested thousands of dollars in the renovation of this plaza. I was also behind on the mortgage payment and the owner was threatening to foreclose on the building. I went to God in prayer and asked God for help. I even cried out to Him as stated in **Philippians 4:6.** I let God know that I needed to pay the mortgage or sell the building to avoid losing my investment.

Approximately two weeks had gone by when a father and son wanted to lease 4000 square feet of space. I only had 3500 square feet left. I told the father and son that I would consider selling the building to them. They purchased the building from me and we closed the transaction two weeks later at their attorney's office. I made a handsome profit from the sale. God answered my prayer.

GOD'S PROMISES

God is always in the life of the believer. He wants the believer to call on Him in time of need.

The bible tells us of God's mercy in the book of Psalm. *"He shall call upon Me, and I will answer him; I will be with him in trouble; I will deliver him and honor him. With long life I will satisfy him, and show him My salvation."* **(Psalm 91:15-16)**

THE PROMISE THAT GOD'S MERCY IS EVERLASTING

The believer can be certain that God's mercy will endure to all generations.

The scripture teaches us in **Psalm 100:5;** *"For the Lord is good; His mercy is everlasting, and His truth endures to all generations."*

God speaks of the mercy that He has for His children. His mercy surpasses all understanding and there is no end to it.

Psalm 59:16-17 tells us; *"But I will sing of Your power; yes, I will sing aloud of Your mercy in the morning; for You have been my defense and refuge in the day of my trouble. To You, O my Strength, I will sing praises; for God is my defense, my God of mercy."*

THE PROMISE OF A NEW COVENANT

"I will put my laws in their mind and write them on their hearts; and I will be their God, and they shall be my people. None of them shall teach his neighbor, and none his brother, saying, 'Know the Lord,' for all shall know Me, from the least of them to the greatest of them. For I will be merciful to their unrighteousness,

and their sins and their lawless deeds I will remember no more. In that He says, A new covenant, He has made the first obsolete. Now what is becoming obsolete and growing old is ready to vanish away." **(Hebrews 8:10b-13)**

God has made many covenants with Abraham and we are the descendants and heirs of these covenants.

These covenants are the blessing of God to the descendants.

"Therefore know that the Lord your God, He is God, the faithful God Who keeps covenant and mercy for a thousand generations with those who love Him and keep His commandments." **(Deuteronomy 7:9)**

GOD'S PROMISES

THE PROMISE OF THE CROWN OF LIFE

Every believer will have to face temptation at some time or another. God expects the believer to operate in self-control at all times. God has given the believer the power to overcome temptation.

The scripture teaches us that if we endure temptation and overcome it, we will receive the 'crown of life' because we love Him. It is our reward.

"Blessed is the man who endures temptation; for when he has been approved, he will receive the crown of life which the Lord has promised to those who love Him." (James 1:12)

A True Story: He Cried Out to God to Save His Life

John and his twelve (12) year old son Kevin decided to go boating one afternoon in Lake Michigan. They had only sailed a short distance from the dock area when a strong gush of wind knocked John from the boat into the lake. Kevin knew that his father could not swim so he went to the edge of the boat to jump in. His father screamed no, don't come in! Then John cried out, "Jesus save me!" Something miraculous happened that was unexplainable! It was as if someone placed their arms beneath John's body and carried him to the shore where he was safe. John knew that God had saved his life. He gave thanks to God. Help was called to bring his boat and his son back to the dock.

"Whoever calls on the name of the Lord shall be saved." (Joel 2:32a)

Chapter Twelve:

The Promise of God's Presence

GOD'S PROMISES

THE PROMISE OF GOD'S PRESENCE

God's presence is everywhere. There is nowhere that He does not exist, and everything is before His eyes. Nothing is hidden from God and nothing can hide from Him. God sees everything and He knows everything.

God lives in every believer who has accepted Christ as his or her Lord and Savior. We can never fully understand Him, because He is incomprehensible. But we should trust Him with everything in us. If we abide in Him and His word abides in us, we will always remain in His presence.

"Draw near to God and He will draw near to you." (**James 4:8a**)

"But without faith it is impossible to please Him, for he who comes to God must believe that He is, and that He is a rewarder to those who diligently seek Him." (**Hebrews 11:6**)

"For the Lord will not forsake His people, for His great name's sake, because it has pleased the Lord to make you His people." (**1 Samuel 12:22**)

"But know that the Lord has set apart for Himself him who is godly; the Lord will hear when I call to Him." (**Psalm 4:3**)

It is written:

"Where can I go from Your Spirit? Or where can I flee from Your presence? If I ascend into heaven, You are there; If I make my bed in hell, behold, You are there. If I take the wings of the morning, And dwell in the uttermost parts of the sea, Even there Your hand shall lead me, And Your right hand shall hold me." (**Psalm 139:7-10**)

THE PROMISE OF ANGELS TO WATCH OVER YOU

The believer who has made God his dwelling place and holy refuge has been given angels to watch over him. God will always see to it that His children are safe from danger. Only God knows about danger before it occurs, because God knows everything and nothing is hidden from Him. He promises to care for the believer in every way.

The scripture teaches us in **Psalm 91:9;** *"Because you have made the Lord who is my refuge, even the Most High, your dwelling place, no evil shall befall you, nor shall any plague come near your dwelling; for He shall give His angels charge over you, to keep you in all your ways."*

The scriptures also teach us that we have entertained angels at times when were not even aware of it. God has sent angels to aid the believer in precarious conditions. One of the assignments the angels perform is to respond to the voice of the word of God, which is spoken by the believer.

The bible teaches us in **Hebrews 13:2;** *"Do not forget to entertain strangers, for by so doing some have unwittingly entertained angels."*

God has given angels assignments to minister to the believer and to aid him in various situations. God knows the needs of His children and will always attend to their needs. When a believer faces a helpless situation, God will always be there to help. We must call on Him.

We find in the book of **Hebrews 1:14;** *"Are they not all ministering spirits sent forth to minister for those who will inherit salvation."*

GOD'S PROMISES

THE PROMISE OF AN INTERCESSOR FOR THE BELIEVER

Jesus said in **John 16:33** of the amplified version, *"I have told you these things, so that in Me you may have peace and confidence. In the world, you have tribulations, trials, distress, and frustration, but be of good cheer. For I have overcome the world."*

In essence, Jesus has conquered the world for all believers. Every believer who abides in Christ and Christ in them is a majority in any situation. Without Jesus, every believer will fall short of God's requirements and laws.

Jesus is appointed an intercessor for every believer. In other words, He acts on behalf of the believer. He pleads our case before God. In essence, He acts as a defense attorney for the believer.

Jesus is our intercessor Who sits at the right hand of God. He is always speaking on behalf of the believer to God. The believer must keep in mind that God is always for him, so who can be against him.

It is written:

"Now He who searches the hearts knows what the mind of the Spirit is, because He makes intercession for the saints according to the will of God." (**Romans 8:27**)

THE PROMISE THE DEVIL WILL NOT TOUCH THE BELIEVER

In the book of Zechariah the 2nd chapter, it tells us that God's children are the apple of His eye. And whoever touches His children, God will deal with them because they are off limit to the evil one. God's children may sin at times, but they will not continue to sin, because they are born of God.

"We know that whoever is born of God does not sin; but he who has been born of God keeps himself, and the wicked one does not touch him." (**1 John 5:18***)*

"Therefore submit to God. Resist the devil and he will flee from you." (**James 4:7**)

The Promise God Will Be Your Shield

There will be times in the believer's life when he will need help because of life threatening events. God has promised that He will always come to the believer's aid in a time such as this.

In **Proverbs 30:5,** God's word tells us; *"Every word of God is pure. He is a shield to those who put their trust in Him."*

Many things that come our way in life can harm us. But the power of God's promises will always act as a shield to protect His children.

The scripture teaches in Psalm 18:2 that God has promised to be our rock and shield if we trust in Him, for He is our Master.

I will give Him first place in my heart, for He died that I may live.

The Promise To Know Secret Things

The secret things belong to the Lord God. However, those who fear God have been promised to know the secret things of God.

The scripture teaches us in **Deuteronomy 29:29:** *"The secret things belong to the Lord our God, but those things which are revealed belong to us and to our children forever, that we may do all the words of this law."*

These secret things will be revealed by the Holy Spirit Who dwells in the believer who is abiding in God and God's word is abiding in him. God wants the believer to live a prosperous life and inherit the things that have been promised by God through our forefathers Abraham, Isaac, and Jacob.

The scripture teaches us; *"Who is the man that fears the Lord? Him shall He teach in the way He chooses. He himself shall dwell in prosperity, and his descendants shall inherit the earth."* **(Psalm 25:12-13)**

The secret things of the Lord are with those believers who fear God and have made a commitment to live according to the word of God.

It is written:

"The secret of the Lord is with those who fear Him, and He will show them His covenant." **(Psalm 25:14)**

Chapter Thirteen:

The Promise of Peace and Prosperity

GOD'S PROMISES

THE PROMISE OF PROSPERITY

The bible tells us that God gets pleasure and is happy when His children are prosperous. In God's word, He tells us how to be prosperous and successful. It is God's word and the obedience of God's word that will bring success into the lives of the believer.

"This book of the law shall not depart from your mouth, but you shall meditate in it day and night, that you may observe to do according to all that is written in it. For then you will make your way prosperous, and then you will have good success" **(Joshua 1:8)**

God desires pleasure and prosperity for all His children, if they are abiding in Him and His word is abiding in them. God will always give prosperity to His children who serve Him.

"If they obey and serve Him, they shall spend their days in prosperity, and their years in pleasures." **(Job 36:11)**

Every mother and father delights in seeing his or her children succeed in life. It gives them joy to see their offspring get ahead in their chosen endeavor. Parents will do whatever is necessary to help their children get ahead and prosper in life.

The scripture teaches us that God wants to give good things to His children. He is pleased to see His children excel in the things of life that are in the will of God. Everything that the believer does in life should always glorify God. Whatever he does, he should do it as though he is doing it for the Lord.

The scripture teaches: *"Let the Lord be magnified, who has pleasure in the prosperity of His servant."* **(Psalm 35:27b)**

God will be glorified when one of His servants stands on the promises of God and never quits. So many believers give up on the promises of God too soon. They become impatient. God will always keep His promise. He is the One Who determines the time of all blessings and blessings will surely follow a period of refinement of the character of the believer. God wants every believer to have the character of His Son Jesus Christ, which in essence is the *Fruit of the Spirit'.* **(Galatians 5:22)**

It is the process of seeking God, which triggers the manifestation of God's promises in the life of the believer. It is God Who gives the believer strength and power to continue to stand on His promises. The believer should always be willing to wait on God to make the promises available in his life.

The bible teaches us in **Psalm 68:35b;** *"The God of Israel is He Who gives strength and power to His people."*

God does not tell His children to get counseling from the nonbeliever or the ungodly. He wants to be the counselor and Father to the needs of His children. He wants to be their provider and their strong tower. He will defend and shelter the believer in the time of need.

The scripture teaches us in **Psalm 1:1-3:** *"Blessed is the man who walks not in the counsel of the ungodly, nor stands in the path of sinners, nor sits in the seat of the scornful; but his delight is in the law of the Lord, and in His law he meditates day and night. He shall be like a tree planted by rivers of water, that brings forth its fruit in its season, whose leaf shall not wither; and whatever he does shall prosper."*

All the needs of the believer will be taken care of by the Father. God knows the needs of each of His children and He has promised not to forsake His own. He cares for each of His servants. He also takes care of the animals. He is aware of the needs of every creature on this earth. The bible tells us that we are more valuable than the birds and God cares for them. He will also take care of His children.

GOD'S PROMISES

The scripture teaches us in **Philippians 4:19**: *"And my God shall supply all your needs according to His riches in glory by Christ Jesus."*

It is written in **Isaiah 58:11**:

"The Lord will guide you continually, and satisfy your soul in drought, and strengthen your bones; you shall be like a watered garden, and like a spring of water, whose waters do not fail."

A Promise Of Wealth

God desires to give His children wealth. The bible teaches us that God takes pleasure in the wealth and prosperity of His saints.

The promises of God contain everything the believer will ever need or desire now and in the future. God wants the believer to have all things that are good for him. God will not give a believer anything that is not good for him. He is a loving God and wants the very best for His children. God does not want His children ever to live in a state of lack.

The bible teaches us in **Romans 8:32;** *"He Who did not spare His own Son, but delivered Him up for us all, how shall He not with Him also freely give us all things."*

No one can accumulate wealth in this world without some measure of power. God is the source of all human power and it is God Who gives one the power to get wealth.

In **Deuteronomy 8:18** it says; *"And you shall remember the Lord your God, for it is He Who gives you power to get wealth, that He may establish His covenant which He swore to your fathers, as it is this day."*

The Promise of Peace and Prosperity

It is the blessing of the Lord, which makes one wealthy. For God holds the key to all wealth in His hand. When a believer has the ability to receive all of God's promises with joy, he is a wealthy person, not the world's way, but God's way. And remember that before God releases wealth in a believer's life, there will be a period of refinement of character.

God gets the glory when one of His children has learned how to stand on the promises of God for his needs and desires. God wants His children to be successful in the things of God more than the believer desires to be successful. Any need or desire of the believer will be sifted through God's will for his life.

God is not glorified when His saints are living in a state of lack. God gets glory in the true manifestation of His children standing on the promises of God and receiving their blessings through the promises.

God wants His children to be obedient to His word and seek Him and His kingdom with everything that is within them. This seeking will activate God's training, refining, molding and finally, the awesome 'Blessing of God's promises.'

Matthew 6:33 teaches; *"But seek first the kingdom of God and His righteousness, and all these things shall be added to you."*

God wants the believer to have the necessary things he needs in life, as well as those things that he desires that are good for him in God's view as well.

The believer must understand that there are two kinds of wealth; the world's wealth and the wealth that the bible is talking about which is God's wealth.

The world defines wealth as a large sum of money, property, or assets. But these things are fleeting and temporal. They may be here today and gone tomorrow. The bible defines wealth as peace, kindness, gentleness, longsuffering, self-control, faithfulness, love, goodness, joy, good health, and all the other promises of God, which also includes money. Money by itself cannot guarantee good health and longevity. Money has many shortcomings. God's wealth has no limitations.

Proverbs 13:22 teaches; *"A good man leaves an inheritance to his children's children, but the wealth of the sinner is stored up for the righteous."*

Ecclesiastes 2:26: *"For God gives wisdom and knowledge and joy to a man who is good in His sight; but to the sinner He gives the work of gathering and collecting, that he may give to him who is good before God."*

Proverbs 8:18-21: *"Riches and honor are with Me, enduring riches and righteousness. My fruit is better than gold, yes, than fine gold, and My revenue than choice silver. I traverse the way of righteousness, in the midst of the paths of justice, that I may cause those who love Me to inherit wealth, that I may fill their treasures."*

A Prayer Of Thanks For The Promise Of Wealth

Father,

You are our provider and helper. You provide every need for Your children. Our trust is in You Father and Your promises. You faithfully see to it that Your blessings flow to us on a daily basis. We are the clay and You are the Potter. You have shaped us to do Your will and follow You. Help us to do this in Jesus' name.

Amen.

A PROMISE OF SUCCESS

Success means accomplishing what one sets out to accomplish or achieving something without infringing on the rights of others. A biblical definition of success could be to follow instructions from God in everything you do. The word of God is primarily instructions, commands, promises, and principles. When the believer follows the teaching of the word of God for success, he will have success in several ways; family, health, wealth and spirit.

The bible teaches us in **Mark 11:23;** *"For assuredly, I say to you, whoever says to this mountain, 'Be removed and be cast into the sea' and does not doubt in his heart, but believe those things he says will be done, he will have whatever he says."*

This is success God's way because an important principle is used here. This believer is imitating God and God accomplished things by speaking them into existence.

In **Genesis 1:3;** *"God said let there be light"; and there was light."*

God wants His children to imitate Him always. In fact, He encourages it. In **Ephesians 5:1** it says; *"Therefore be imitators of God as dear children."*

Success means doing the best we can with what we have. Success is a personal standard of reaching for the highest that is in us, and becoming all that we can be with God as our source and strength.

God wants all of His children to succeed. In fact, He wants us to succeed more than we want success for ourselves. God gets the glory when one of His children stands on His promises and gains success. God is not glorified when one of His children fails.

As the believer becomes productive in his chosen field, success is assured when he is abiding in Jesus Christ. The scripture teaches us in **John 15:5;** *"I am the vine, you are the branches. He who abides in Me, and I in him, bears much fruit; for without Me you can do nothing."*

So the answer to success for a believer is to always abide in Jesus and live a life of obedience to the word of God.

The bible also teaches the believer where success really comes from. It comes from wisdom. The bible also encourages us to get wisdom, for it is the principle thing.

Finally, we must pray for success as we learn from a biblical character in the Old Testament.

In **Genesis 24:12,** we find Abraham's servant praying for success in going to another city to find Abraham's son a wife. Then he said, *"Oh Lord God of my master Abraham, please give me success this day, and show kindness to my master Abraham."* God answered the servant's prayer and the servant brought back Rachel from a city called Nahor in Mesopotamia. Abraham's son Isaac and Rachel were later married.

"All things are possible for the believer who believes." **(Mark 9:23).**

It is God Who gives the believer power to become successful. It is totally up to the believer to make his way successful by operating in faith and standing on the promises of God. The bible gives instructions, commandments, laws, and principles that the believer should use to become successful God's way. God requires the believer to use faith to become successful.

The bible teaches us that without faith it is impossible to please God **(Hebrews 11:6).**

The believer should not only have faith in God and His word, but he should have sufficient belief in himself also. He should see himself as God sees him.

God sees His children as winners and conquerors. He has given His children strength and power to become successful.

The Promise of Peace and Prosperity

Remember, success God's way is not success according to the world's definition of success. Again, success God's way is health, prosperity, family, and spirit. The believer has something that the unbeliever does not have and that is the promises of God that he can always rely on.

The unbeliever does not have the privilege of relying on and depending on the promises of God because he has separated himself from God by not being in the family of God. He must repent of his sins, confess, and believe that Jesus died on the cross for him and that God raised Him from the dead. He must ask Jesus to come into his heart and be his Savior.

Once the unbeliever does this, he is now in the family of God and has eternal life. He is now eligible for the promises of God. He is no longer separated from God but belongs to God and is a child of God. A person who has achieved an abundance of money, fame and lost his family in a divorce is not successful God's way. The bible tells us that God hates divorce.

The bible gives the believer instructions on how to become successful. **Joshua 1:8** tells us; *"This book of the law shall not depart from your mouth, but you shall meditate in it day and night, that you may observe to do accordingly to all that is written in it. For then you will make your way prosperous, and then you will have good success."*

To become successful God's way will require faith, diligence, and work. There is no other way to achieve success. God will not make a believer successful, but God will give the believer the power and strength to become successful. However, he must seek first the kingdom of God and success will be one of the benefits.

God has already placed inside every human being the necessary ingredients to become what God envisioned him to be. The ultimate purpose of the believer is to glorify God through the service that God has called him to do. The service, which God has called the believer to do, is his earthly assignment.

The promises that God has made to His children are designed to give life, joy, hope, and happiness forever for the believer. Without God and His promises, there can be no hope for the future, for He is the believer's life.

A Promise To Be The Lender And Not The Borrower

For the obedient believer who carefully follows all of God's commands, all blessings will come upon him. Prosperity and wealth will be in his house. The favor of the Lord is with him and his family.

God truly wants the believer to have wealth in his house. In fact, God wants wealth for the believer more than the believer wants wealth for himself. Remember, God is only glorified when His children display prosperity here on earth. God said in the scripture that He would be glorified through His children only. So when one of God's children lives in lack, do you think God is glorified? Indeed not. God will not be glorified in the believer's life until the believer is prosperous.

"The Lord will open to you His good treasure, the heavens, to give the rain to your land in its season, and to bless all the work of your hand. You shall lend to many nations, but you shall not borrow." **(Deuteronomy 28:12)**

Ask In The Name Of Jesus

The bible teaches us in **John 15:7;** *"If you abide in Me, and My words abide in you, you will ask what you desire, and it shall be done for you."*

Anything that we as believers ask God for must be in His will for us. When what we ask for is in God's will, He hears us, and if He hears us, whatever we ask for will be granted.

The Promise of Peace and Prosperity

The believer must remember that when he receives anything from God in the name of Jesus, God is glorified because the believer bears fruit.

God is glorified each time one of His children receives fruit because of the prayer of faith through His Son, Jesus Christ.

It gives God pleasure when one of His servants is prosperous. And it pleases God when one of His servants uses faith in prayer and deed.

God wants His children to have success and be productive in this life. He wants to give us good gifts and help us with our goals and desires. Why? He is a God of love. He is always showing His love to His children, even when we are not aware of it. The bible compares gifts given by an earthly unsaved father to his children and God's gifts to His children: *"If you then, being evil, know how to give good gifts to your children, how much more will your Father Who is in heaven give good things to those who ask Him!"* (**Matthew 7:11**)

"And whatever you ask in My name, that I will do, that the Father may be glorified in the Son." (**John 14:13**)

"And whatever things you ask in prayer, believing, you will receive." (**Matthew 21:22**)

It pleases God to give His children good things when they are obedient. God does not desire to withhold any good thing from His children; He wants His children to call upon Him and seek Him.

The Lord is near to all who call upon Him. The scripture teaches us that He is always close to us to watch over us and hear our cry. He will protect us and provide for us.

"To all who call upon Him in truth, He will fulfill the desire of those who fear Him." (**Psalm 145:18b-19**)

113

GOD'S PROMISES

God always knows the needs of His children. He wants to give His children all things that are good for them in accordance to His will.

Every human being on the face of the earth has desires. Some desires are small and some are large. Desires are an innate part of the human existence. God made man and gave them the capacity to have desires. Our hope is based on our desires. Without hope, there is no real basis to live. The incentive to live is based on our desires, our hope, and our loved ones.

The bible tells us that God will give us what we ask, if what we do, pleases Him. It pleases God when His children trust and obey Him. He delights in giving His children the things that they desire. The very first step in pleasing God is to make a commitment to follow Jesus Christ. The second step is to apply faith in everything we do. The bible tells us that without faith we cannot please God.

The scripture tells us in **1 John** that we will receive what we ask for.

"And whatever we ask we receive from Him, because we keep His commandments and do those things that are pleasing in His sight." **(1 John 3:22)**

A Promise To Preserve The Believer From Evil

The scriptures teach us that; *"The Lord shall preserve you from all evil; He shall preserve your soul."* **(Psalm 121:7)**

This teaching is to give knowledge to the believer that God will keep him safe in all aspects of his life forever. No evil can touch God's children because of this promise. The believer's soul is off limits to the devil. However, this promise, just like all of God's promises, comes with a price.

There are conditions that I will limit at this point:

- The believer must be committed to God.
- The believer must be in the process of seeking God diligently.

Chapter Fourteen:

The Promise of Confidence in Jesus

GOD'S PROMISES

A PROMISE ALL THINGS ARE POSSIBLE IF YOU BELIEVE

Nothing that is common to man will be impossible for a believer to achieve if it is the will of God. I believe whatever God allows the believer to imagine, he can achieve. He only needs the strength of Jesus to make it happen.

I do believe that when a believer is abiding in God and God is abiding in him, he can produce great things. If the believer has sufficient faith, and it is the will of God, nothing is impossible to him.

The bible does not teach any limits for the believer who fears God and delights greatly in His commands. For God placed some of His own attributes in the believer to perform great things here on earth through Christ.

The scriptures teach that we can do the things that Jesus did when He walked on the earth. If we could not do them, He would not have said we could.

The bible teaches this in **John 14:12;** *"Most assuredly, I say to you, he who believes in Me, the works that I do he will do also, and greater works than these he will do, because I go to my Father."*

The only reason that a believer cannot do some of the things Jesus did here on earth is because of a lack of belief. Jesus has reminded the believer that with a little faith, nothing would be impossible to him.

In **Matthew 17:20** it teaches us this truth: *"So Jesus said to them, because of your unbelief, for assuredly I say to you, if you have faith as a mustard seed, you will say to this mountain, move from here to there and it will move, and nothing will be impossible for you."*

Whenever a believer has a problem in his life, he can stand on this promise and command the problem to move. But you must keep one thing

116

in mind—you as a believer must be totally committed to God, otherwise it will not happen. When you are in this special relationship with Jesus, you can indeed speak with authority to any problem and stand on this promise in Matthew 17:20 and you shall have what you say. If the mountain does not move in time, God may be teaching you patience, so just continue to wait on God. He will not let you down. The bible says that the believer who is trusting in God will not be put to shame. In other words, God will honor your trust in Him.

Nothing in the will of God is impossible for the believer who is abiding in God and the word of God is abiding in him. God does not hold back or prevent something from being manifested in the believer's life when His requirements are met. However, some things that are desired in the life of the believer are not good for the believer. Consequently, these desires will not be honored by God. God only allows the believer to do what he can see himself doing. This is the power of the imagination, which is God's gift to all mankind.

Jesus said; *"If you can believe, all things are possible to him who believes."* **(Mark 9:23)**

Jesus did what some people thought as the impossible while He was on earth. Before He left the earth, He promised the disciples that they could do the same things, and even greater things they could do, because He would go to His Father in heaven. The things that Jesus did on earth were the works that the Father gave Him to do.

We as believers have been given the favor of God, simply because we are in the family of God and we are committed to Him and all His ways.

When we stand on God's promises and allow God to prepare us to receive His promises, this is where God begins to work in the believer's life.

God begins to reshape our lives by molding us to be like His Son Jesus. Our character is so important to God. If there is a flaw in the character of the believer, God will refine the character before any promise is manifested in the believer's life. Once the believers character is satisfactory to God, (not necessarily perfect), God will allow -- begin to manifest His promises in the life of the believer.

DEATH AND LIFE ARE IN THE
POWER OF THE TONGUE

"Death and life are in the power of the tongue, and those who love it will eat its fruit." **(Proverbs 18:21)**

Our words have power that is beyond our imagination. When the believer speaks, he gives his words power to be a seed planted here on earth. This word that was spoken will perform as a fruit of its kind and will promote life or death to the speaker in the long run.

If the words of the speaker are spoken for a length of time, his words will become manifested in like-kind in the life of the believer. Thus, one should never dwell on or say the following:

- I don't feel good

- I have no future

- I don't like this person

- I am broke or I am poor

- I can't understand the bible

- I will never be successful

The Promise of Confidence in Jesus

- I will never be prosperous

- I cannot forgive what he/she did to me

- I will never be wealthy

- I think I'm going to be sick

- I cannot do or learn something, etc.

One should always meditate on and repeat the following:

- I can do all things through Christ Who strengthens me.

- God is my provider whenever there is a need.

- God is my helper in time of trouble.

- God will always honor His word and keep me and my family safe.

- God is my Rock. I will not be moved.

- God promises to preserve my life.

- God will direct my steps if I always acknowledge Him first.

- God controls everything that comes my way. Why should I worry?

- I am God's child. He will take care of me and my family.

- God loves me and my family.

GOD'S PROMISES

THE LORD PROMISES THE BELIEVER
THAT HE WILL BE THE BELIEVER'S CONFIDENCE

"Do not be afraid of sudden terror, nor of trouble from the wicked when it comes. For the Lord will be your confidence and will keep your foot from being caught." **(Proverbs 3:25-26)**

To be victorious in this life, the believer must demonstrate a spirit of confidence. However, this confidence should come through Jesus Himself. Why? Jesus has promised us to be our confidence when we call on Him for His aid. The believer has a right to be bold in life because of the confidence he has placed in His Savior, Jesus Christ.

A PROMISE TO GIVE STRENGTH TO THE BELIEVER

The bible teaches us throughout, God is our everything. We need God for everything. In fact, God wants the believer to depend on Him for everything.

In the book of John, it tells us that without Jesus we can do nothing. *"I am the Vine, you are the branches. He who abides in Me, and I in him, bears much fruit, for without Me you can do nothing."* **(John 15:5)**

The believer's ability to perform well in any task, depends on God Himself. All of our power comes from God. God is the source of power that we have and we must ask Him to empower us and He will give us what we ask.

It is written:

"Oh God, You are more awesome than Your holy places. The God of Israel is He Who gives strength and power to His people, Blessed be God!" **(Psalm 68:35)**

The Promise of Confidence in Jesus

The believer can ask God for strength at anytime. He will give strength to the believer instantly. When the believer depends on God for everything, he actually puts God first, and foremost in his life. God wants to be first in every believer's life. Nothing should be placed before God! Anything you place before God is your master. A believer cannot have two masters. The bible teaches us that we will love one and hate the other.

When the believer is abiding in God's word and the word of God is abiding in the believer, he can ask for anything and God will hear him. If it is according to the will of God, the believer must believe that he has already received it and he will have it.

It is written: *"Behold God is my salvation, I will trust and not be afraid; For the Lord, is my strength and song; He also has become my salvation."* **(Isaiah 12:2)**

It is God Who gives strength to the believer. If a person does not have strength, he is not able to perform his tasks. God is always ready to give a believer the strength he needs.

The scripture teaches us; *"Fear not, for I am with you; be not dismayed, for I am your God. I will strengthen you, yes, I will help you, I will uphold you with My righteous right hand."* **(Isaiah 41:10)**

There will be times in the believer's life when he will need power to accomplish certain things in life.

Remember this, God is the One Who gives His people strength.

The bible teaches us in **Philippians 4:13;** *"I can do all things through Christ Who strengthens me."*

It is unlimited what a believer can do who is abiding in God and depending on Him for power and strength.

The bible teaches us in **2 Timothy 1:7** that fear does not come from God.

"For God has not given us a spirit of fear, but of power and of love and of a sound mind."

In **Psalm 27:14,** this scripture teaches us to be ready, always to wait on the Lord. *"Wait on the Lord; be of good courage, and He shall strengthen your heart; wait, I say, on the Lord!"*

It is written: *"Be of good courage, and He shall strengthen your heart, all you who hope in the Lord."* **(Psalm 31:24)**

God has promised to give strength to the believer when he is weak. He is always merciful and He never changes. He gave strength to the people of Israel to make them strong at the exact moment they needed it.

Every child of God will at times experience weakness and sorrow of heart. There is something about the flesh, that at times becomes weary and dismayed. This is the time that God's word will strengthen us to show Himself strong in us. This is the time that the believer can call on the Father for strength. He will always hear our prayer. God is always there to console us and comfort us when we are lowly in our spirit.

Chapter Fifteen:

The Promise of God to Manifest Himself

GOD'S PROMISES

God's Promise To Those Who Keep His Commandments

"If you love Me, keep My commandments." (**John 14:15**)

"He who has My commandments and keeps them, it is he who loves Me. And he who loves Me will be loved by My Father, and I will love him and manifest Myself to him." (**John 14:21**)

The believer's love toward God is demonstrated by the believer keeping the commandments of God. When the believer lives by God's commandments, he is in obedience to the word of God and God promises to manifest Himself to the believer who keeps His commandments.

God has also promised to give many blessings to those who obey His commandments. Belief and obedience are the basis of all the promises being released in the life of the believer.

Promises To The Believer's Descendants

The believer who trusts in the Lord, and abides in His word, can expect many blessings that God has promised to His children. God has promised to bless the descendants down to many generations. This is the love that God has for His children and His children's children.

God loves the believer who keeps His commandments. His word says that He will bless those who keep His commandments. The believer's children will also benefit from their parents obedience to the word of God. For God's commandments are not gruesome or overbearing. They are but a small price to pay for the value of God's promises and the things that God has in store for the believer who remains faithful to the end.

The Promise of God to Manifest Himself

The scripture tells us that no eyes have seen nor ears have heard of the things that God has prepared for those who love Him. The believer's life that he is living today is only a small investment for the eternal life that God has promised him when Jesus returns for His saints.

The scripture teaches us in **Psalm 112:1-3:** *"Blessed is the man who fears the Lord, who delights greatly in His commandments. His descendants will be mighty on earth; the generation of the upright will be blessed. Wealth and riches will be in his house, and his righteousness endures forever."*

"For I will pour water on him who is thirsty, and floods on the dry ground; I will pour my Spirit on your descendants, and My blessing on your offspring." **(Isaiah 44:3)**

GOD'S PROMISE TO POUR OUT HIS SPIRIT
UPON ALL FLESH

The bible teaches us in **John 3:16:** *"For God so loved the world that He gave His only begotten Son, that whoever believes in Him should not perish but have everlasting life."*

The scripture also teaches us that it is not the will of God that any should perish, but that all would come to repentance of their sins. God will always have His way and He will always do what is pleasing to Him.

God's word tells us that in the last days God will pour out His Spirit upon all flesh to cause man to repent and accept His Son Jesus Christ. This act of God will be a final act of the love of God for mankind.

This is the word that was spoken by the prophet Joel; *"And it shall come to pass afterward that I will pour out My Spirit on all flesh; your sons and daughters shall prophesy, your old men shall dream dreams, your young men shall see visions."* **(Joel 2:28)**

GOD'S PROMISES

GOD HAS PROMISED NOT TO FORGET HIS SAINTS

The bible teaches us that God's love is so great for the world that He gave His only Son to die for all of mankind. The death of Jesus demonstrated the love God has for each one of His children. Every believer is a cherished child of God and He has promised to never forsake or leave him or her. He said that He would always be with them to care for them and be a shield to protect them.

The promises that God has made to the believers are binding and can never be broken. All of God's promises are yes to the believer who remains in the word of God and the word of God remains in him. As the believer trusts in God, he is molded and shaped into the character of Jesus Christ, for this is the will of God.

The scripture teaches in **Isaiah 49:15-16;** *"Can a woman forget her nursing child, and not have compassion on the son of her womb? Surely, they may forget, yet I will not forget you. See, I have inscribed you on the palms of My hands; your walls are continually before me."*

A MAN'S STOMACH

SHALL BE SATISFIED BY WHAT HE IS CONFESSING

The power of the spoken word is a seed planted by the one who sows it. Each time the believer speaks, he is planting a seed into his life that will be manifested in the future. We will become in time, what we believe and what we are confessing. Our thoughts build our future because our thoughts are unspoken words that clothe themselves in action, and action leads to decisions which shape our lives.

The Promise of God to Manifest Himself

The scripture tells us in **Proverbs 23:7;** *"As a man thinks, so is he."*

In time, a man becomes what he thinks about all the time. His dominant thought is the driving force that gives direction to where he is headed in life. Our thoughts will always precede our actions. This is the way God designed us and this is the way it will be. Our actions will determine our direction and our direction in life will determine our destination.

The message of God's word is to inform the believer to think and have the mindset of God; to think His thoughts, to love the things He loves and to despise sin the way He does. The word of God can change the believer's thoughts which will guide his ways and actions.

God loves righteousness and He hates sin. The intent of God's word is to have the believer to love righteousness and to hate sin. This is the true mindset of God. This is what will happen to the believer when he seeks God with everything that is in him. The end result is for the believer to be like Jesus and love the things He loves and hate the things He hates. For Jesus hated unrighteousness and He displayed a love for people.

God has designed the believer to experience the things in life that he is confessing. If the believer is confessing the word of God **(Philippians 4:19)** which says; *"My God shall supply all of my needs according to His riches in glory by Christ Jesus;"* here the believer will receive what he is confessing. All of God's teachings support his beliefs. If on the other hand, the believer is confessing that he does not believe that God will supply all of his needs, he will have what he is confessing.

Belief is the deciding factor that gives God's word power. It is faith that determines our belief in the word of God. God's word teaches us in the book of **Proverbs 18:20;** *"A man's stomach shall be satisfied from the fruit of his mouth; from the produce of his lips he shall be filled."*

Chapter Sixteen:

The Promise to Those Who Seek God

GOD'S PROMISES

A Promise To Those Who Seek God

"But seek first the Kingdom of God and His righteousness, and all these things shall be added to you." (**Matthew 6:33**)

All believers have needs, desires, dreams and hopes that God is very much aware of, and God wants to give the believer the desires of his heart. But God wants the believer to put things into perspective first, so that all these things will not control him. God is saying to first seek Him and all these things will be added to the life of the believer.

The scriptures tell us that we must continue to seek and we will find; *"So I say to you, ask, and it will be given to you; seek, and you will find; knock, and it will be opened to you."* (**Luke 11:9**)

The Power Of The Believer's Spoken Word

It is a known fact that the words that we speak will shape our lives and affect the lives of those around us. Our thoughts, words, and actions will define our life and give meaning to our future.

All of our actions begin with the power of a single thought, and every word that is spoken must begin with a thought. God designed our thought process this way and this is the way it will be. There is nothing we can do to change it. Our thoughts are so important to our success and they will clothe themselves to reflect who we are and how others perceive us.

The believer should only confess those things from his heart that he is willing to live with. The believer can define his life by what he is confessing. He should only speak those things about himself that defines who he wants to become.

The Promise to Those Who Seek God

The believer should never confess what he does not desire or what he does not want to live with. He should never say that he is poor or that he feels ill or he has a disease even if there are clear symptoms. We as believers do not confess or agree with anything that does not line up with what the word of God says about us. The word of God teaches us in **Isaiah 53:5;** *"By his stripes we are healed."*

We must always confess the word of God by saying that we are healed, no matter what the symptoms reveal. A symptom is not a sickness nor a disease.

The bible also teaches us that we shall have what we say; *"For assuredly, I say to you, whoever says to this mountain, 'Be removed and be cast into the sea,' and does not doubt in his heart, but believes that these things he says will be done, he will have whatever he says."* **(Mark 11:23)**

Our words have more power than we think, and when we speak, we are planting thought seeds in our minds or someone else's mind. These seeds in time will cause things to happen, either for good or for bad. We should always make sure to speak 'good' things about ourselves and others.

The scripture teaches us; *"Call those things that do not exist, as though they do."* **(Romans 4:17)**

We can speak certain things into our lives by constantly confessing them over and over again. In time what we have been confessing will manifest itself into our lives.

Even our health can be affected by what we are confessing. Our bodies and its functions are directly linked to what we are confessing with our mouth.

It is written:

"There is one who speaks like the piercings of a sword, but the tongue of the wise promotes health." **(Proverbs 12:18)**

GOD'S PROMISES

The bible teaches that we can promote good health in our body by speaking words of health, and consequently, our body will respond to what is being spoken. This is the way God has designed us and the way we should relate to our body. And remember, our actions follow our speaking and our speaking follows our thinking.

The scripture teaches us that; *"In the beginning was the Word, and the Word was with God, and the Word was God."* **(John 1:1)**

The scripture teaches us that Jesus is the word and He was with God in the beginning, and Jesus is God!

The scripture teaches us in **Genesis 1:3**; *"Then God said, 'Let there be light'; and there was light."*

The scripture tells us that everything that was made including light, was made by the invisible word of God.

The believer is to always embrace the word of God and keep it on his tongue at all times. The word of God is everything to the saints of God.

It is written in **Proverbs 4:20-22**; *"My son, give attention to my words; incline your ear to my sayings. Do not let them depart from your eyes; keep them in the midst of your heart; for they are life to those who find them, and health to all their flesh."*

God's word will still be alive, even when the heavens and earth no longer exist.

"Heaven and earth will pass away, but My words will by no means pass away." **(Matthew 24:35)**

"The grass withers, the flower fades, but the word of our God stands forever." **(Isaiah 40:8)**

"For the word of God is living and powerful, and sharper than any two-edged sword, piercing even to the division of soul and spirit, and of joints and marrow, and is a discerner of the thoughts and intents of the heart." **(Hebrews 4:12)**

This scripture teaches us that God is a discerner of the thoughts and intents of the heart. His word is very much alive and is very powerful.

"By the word of the Lord the heavens were made, and all the host of them by the breath of His mouth." **(Psalm 33:6)**

I have often heard people say things like "I feel like I am going to lose this battle," or "I don't think I will ever pass this test," or "I don't think she likes me." As a believer, however, you should always examine thoughts and statements such as these, because these words have power and consequences.

A believer should only say what he wants to live with. Why? His word is like a seed. It will show up later to visit the believer. If you do not want what you confess, then do not say it.

"A man will be satisfied with good by the fruit of his mouth. And the recompense of a man's hands will be rendered to him." **(Proverbs 12:14)**

All spoken words in the spiritual realm are like seeds planted in a garden. They will one day come up to fulfill their assignment.

Jesus demonstrated the power of the spoken word when He cursed the fig tree.

In **Matthew 21:19-22** it says; *"And seeing a fig tree by the road, He (Jesus) came to it and found nothing on it but leaves, and said to it; 'Let no fruit grow on you ever again.' Immediately the fig tree withered away. And when the disciples saw it, they marveled, saying, 'How did the fig tree wither away so soon?'"*

So Jesus answered and said to them, *"Assuredly, I say to you, if you have faith and do not doubt, you will not only do what was done to the fig tree, but also if you say to this mountain, 'Be removed and be cast into the sea,' it will be done. And whatever things you ask in prayer, believing, you will receive."*

We, as God's children, must remember that the words we speak have power and therefore, consequences. Our words when spoken, go out into the earth and will act as a seed planted in our life. These 'word seeds' will manifest themselves into our lives later.

The bible tells us in Romans that the believer can call things into his life by his spoken words. The believer must also be aware that the things he profess must be in the will of the Father for his life. The scripture teaches us that faith is the substance of things hoped for and is the evidence of things not seen.

In essence, if you repeat something over and over again, you will eventually not only believe it, but you will hope for it, subconsciously. Remember, faith comes by hearing something over and over again.

A PROMISE TO THOSE WHO WAIT ON GOD

When God makes a promise to the believer, He will always honor the promise. His promise is His word and we can depend on the promises of God to be manifested. However, no one knows when the promise will come but God Himself. There may be some occasions where God will give a believer a time and date, but it is solely up to God to manifest a date and time. Usually this information belongs to God Himself. However, there is a price to pay for the promises. They are not 'free' as some may think. Here is a list of part of the price that must be paid by the believer to receive the promises of God:

- Patience, self-control, total commitment, faith, trust
- Flawless character, belief, seeking God's kingdom
- Obedience, decreeing the promises to be manifested

The Promise to Those Who Seek God

There are over 4000 promises in the bible, both implicit and explicit. The value of these promises is more than all the silver, gold and money in the entire world! Therefore, the promises of God are worth waiting for.

During the waiting period, God will use this time wisely to train the believer. The time that the believer is waiting on God is not wasted time. God is using this time to mold, shape and refine the believer's character to be like His Son Jesus and to conform the believer to His commandments. This period of shaping, molding and refining the believer's character will cause some suffering. However, the suffering is controlled by God. He knows how much we can bear.

Waiting on God can be one of the most difficult things in life for the believer. Waiting is a task that goes against the flesh of the believer. No one loves to wait, but we can learn to wait patiently with the help of God Who gives us strength. We only need to ask Him and He will give us the strength to wait patiently. Waiting is basically trust and self-control in the promises of God. It is also the fruit of the spirit. The flesh is always against waiting. When the believer is abiding in the word of God and God's word is abiding in him, in time the Spirit will bring the flesh under control.

There is always a blessing to the believer who waits on the Lord. The scripture teaches us not to envy others who prosper in their ways, but to trust in the Lord. God only asks us to delight ourselves in Him.

"Delight yourself also in the Lord, and He shall give you the desires of your heart." **(Psalm 37:4)**

Only God knows all the reasons why He makes the believer wait. However, we do know that faith is increased through the process of waiting. The believer's trust is also increased through the period of waiting.

GOD'S PROMISES

The scripture teaches us that good will always come to the believer who waits for God.

"For since the beginning of the world men have not heard nor perceived by the ear, nor has the eye seen any God besides You, Who acts for the one who waits for Him." **(Isaiah 64:4)**. We can discover God's will and purpose for our life as we seek the kingdom of God and wait on Him. God is actively working in the believer's life during this period of waiting.

The scripture tells us in the book of Lamentations; *"The Lord is good to those who wait for Him, to the soul who seeks Him."* **(Lamentations 3:25)**

The scripture teaches us that God will supply power and strength to those who need it if only they would wait for Him. In the book of Isaiah, it tells us; *"He gives power to the weak, and to those who have no might, He increases strength. Even the youths shall faint and be weary, and the young men shall utterly fall, but those who wait on the Lord shall renew their strength; they shall mount up with wings like eagles, they shall run and not be weary, they shall walk and not faint."* **(Isaiah 40:29-31)**

A Promise To Give Direction

"Show me Your ways, O Lord, teach me Your paths; Guide me in Your truth and teach me, for You are God my Savior, and my hope is in You all day long. Remember, O Lord, Your great mercy and love, for They are from of old." **(Psalm 25:4-6NIV)**

Every person on the face of this planet will need direction during some point in life. All people will make the wrong decision at various times in life.

The future is an unknown to all people. Only God knows the future. He knows the outcome of every event or meeting before it ever takes place.

Through prayer, we can ask God to lead us and He will direct us in the best way to go. God is always available and delights in leading the way of the believer. All the believer has to do is ask God for directions and God will direct his path.

The scripture teaches us in **Proverbs 3:5-6;** *"Trust in the Lord with all your heart, and lean not on your own understanding; in all your ways acknowledge Him, and He shall direct your paths."*

I believe that this promise can prevent the believer from being involved in an accident if he prays this prayer before taking a trip, whether by airplane, train, cruise ship/boat or automobile. Accidents are happening every hour and every day across the country. God is aware of every one of these accidents long before it happens. When you ask God for directions, do you believe that He will direct you into the path of one of these accidents? God will not direct you into the path of an accident when you have asked Him to direct you. He knows every believer who is totally committed to Him.

God will always honor His promises to His children. He delights in seeing His children have a safe journey while traveling. The bible teaches us that the believer will plan his way, but God will direct his every step. **(Proverbs 16:9)**

John 8:12 tells us; *"Then Jesus spoke to them again, saying, "I am the light of the world. He who follows Me shall not walk in darkness, but have the light of life."*

GOD'S PROMISES

A Prayer For The Promise Of Your Guidance

Father,

Your word says to acknowledge You in everything that I do and You will direct my paths. I am about to take a trip and I am trusting You to direct my path safely to my destination. Thank You Father! In Jesus name I pray,

Amen.

A Promise To Be An Over-Comer

"For whatever is born of God overcomes the world. And this is the victory that has overcome the world—our faith." (**1 John 5:4**)

"Who is he who overcomes the world, but he who believes that Jesus is the Son of God." (**1 John 5:5**)

The scriptures teach us that: *"Him who overcomes I will make a pillar in the temple of my God."* (**Rev. 3:12 NIV**)

The scripture teaches us in **Rev. 3:21**; *"To him who overcomes; I will give the right to sit with me on my throne, just as I overcame and sat down with My Father on His throne."* The scripture teaches us in **Rev. 2:26(NIV)**; *"To him who overcomes and does my will to the end, I will give authority over the nations."*

The scripture teaches us in **Rev. 2:7b(NIV)**; *"To him who overcomes, I will give the right to eat from the tree of life, which is in the paradise of God."*

Jesus overcame the world and we as His followers are to do likewise. God gives His children the power to be over-comers. When the believer needs help, he can ask God for power to overcome any situation that he is faced with.

There was a pastor who once said, "The biggest battles are fought and won on your knees."

God has already given His children the victory before the battle has ever begun. God will teach His children how to overcome by sending trials in their lives. Each trial sent is a test to strengthen the believer in several ways:

- Increased faith

- Increased trust

- Increased belief

A True Story: Joan Spoke to Her Disabled Car

On Monday morning as Joan was about to leave for work, she started her car and drove out of the driveway. As soon as she proceeded onto the street, suddenly the car turned off. She left the car on the side of the street and walked back to the house and told her husband what had happened. She told him that she didn't feel that it was safe to drive the car to work which was more than a two hour drive because the car might stop on her again. Her husband told her to speak to the car and decree that it would not malfunction ever again while she was driving. Joan went to her car and spoke to the car the exact words her husband told her to say and she drove to work without any trouble with the car. The car never malfunctioned again. Joan knew that God had answered her prayers. She and her husband Frank are strong believers in God and His promises. Frank knows that God will always honor His promises. He stood on the promise of God in **Mark 11:23** which says; *"Whoever says to this mountain be thou removed and cast into the sea and does not doubt in his heart but believes those things which he says will be done; he shall have what he says."*

139

All believers should always remember that the word of God is alive and very powerful. This teaching can be found in Hebrews the fourth chapter and twelfth verse.

A True Story: A Lady Confesses That Someday Someone Would Kill Her

A young man in his teens was walking down the sidewalk in a community of a small town. In his own words, he said that something lured him into this house where an elderly woman lived. He stated that he heard voices and was told to go into this house and kill the old woman. She was sitting in her recliner. The young man entered her front door which was not locked and killed the woman. He confessed later to his parents and the authorities that he did not know why he killed the lady but it was as though he was driven uncontrollably to obey the voice inside his head. He did not know the lady.

After the woman's death her children said that their mother had previously told them about how she had feared that someone would one day break in her home and kill her. They said that she lived in constant fear and believed that this would happen to her.

The woman believed and even expected to be killed, so much so, that she told her children she felt that she was going to be killed.

A person should never decree anything that he doesn't want in his life. The spoken word is very powerful. There is a saying: "If you don't want it to happen, don't say it."

Job 3:25 tells us: *"For the thing I greatly feared has come upon me."* The scriptures teach us in **Proverbs 18:21:** *"Death and life are in the power of the tongue, and those who love it will eat its fruit."*

Chapter Seventeen:

The Promise of Special Blessing

GOD'S PROMISES

A Promise Of Blessings To The Believer

God has blessed His children with many blessings and will continue to bless them because of His love for them. The bible tells us that God is love and His love is everlasting.

The bible says that God loved the world so much that He gave His only begotten son to die for the sin of man. This kind of love is beyond comprehension and is called agape love which only God is capable of performing.

As descendants of the Abrahamic covenant, we as believers are the recepients of the following promise:

"Blessing I will bless you, and multiplying I will multiply your descendants as the stars of the heaven and as the sand which is on the seashore; and your descendants shall possess the gate of their enemies. In your seed all the nations of the earth shall be blessed, because you have obeyed My voice." **(Genesis 22:17-18)**

All believers are the direct heir to this promise because of the obedience of Abraham to the voice of God. God has many blessings in store for the believer who is obedient to His commandments and will trust in Him.

In the book of Psalm it tells us the many blessings that we as believers can look forward to when our walk is in alignment with the word of God and we fully trust Him.

"Blessed is the man who walks not in the counsel of the ungodly, nor stands in the path of sinners, nor sits in the seat of the scornful; but his delight is in the law of the Lord, and in His law he meditates day and night. He shall be like a tree planted by rivers of water, that brings forth its fruit in its season, whose leaf also shall not wither; and whatever he does shall prosper. The ungodly are not so, but are like the chaff that the wind drives away. Therefore the ungodly shall not stand in

the judgment, nor sinners in the congregation of the righteous. For the Lord knows the way of the righteous, but the way of the ungodly shall perish." **(Psalm 1:1-6)**

The Lord has promised to bless those who consider the poor:

"Blessed is he who considers the poor; the Lord will deliver him in time of trouble. The Lord will preserve him and keep him alive, and he will be blessed on the earth; You will not deliver him to the will of his enemies. (God will protect Him). The Lord will strengthen him on his bed of illness; You will sustain him on his sickbed." **(Psalm 41:1-3)**

God has put aside special blessings for those who consider the poor. Each time a person helps the poor, it is a seed that is planted for a harvest and God has promised to bless the believer in several ways. A prayer for the poor is also a seed that is planted.

The bible teaches us that he who gives to help the work of God will be blessed with a harvest.

The scripture teaches us in **Genesis 8:22:** *"While the earth remains, seedtime and harvest, cold and heat, winter and summer, and day and night shall not cease."*

God has also promised to bless the work of your hands when you give to the brother who is among you who is destitute or in need. The scripture teaches us not to harden our heart toward the brethren, for if he cries out to God about his needs, this will be counted as a sin against you.

In essence, blessings from the Lord comes from trusting, obedience and faith in God's word. God wants to bless His children with things that are good for them in God's view.

It is written:

"He who did not spare His own Son, but delivered Him up for us all, how shall He not with Him also freely give us all things?" **(Romans 8:32)**

GOD'S PROMISES

A Prayer for the Promise of Blessings

Lord,

You have many blessings in store for Your children, too many for me to count. I am truly blessed to be one of the heirs of the promise. I thank You for all that You have in the future for my well being. You have given me so much to look forward to. I praise You with all that is within me, in Jesus name, and I thank You for this promise of many blessings in my life.

Amen.

God will bless His children with many blessings, because it is His nature to do so. The scripture teaches us that God is love and blessings naturally flow from love. God wants His children to be a blessing to others and that is why He said that of the three gifts, love, faith and hope, the greatest of these is love.

God wants to give the believer the desires of his heart, and He gets pleasure from the prosperity of His servants. The believer will receive so many blessings from God on a daily basis, it is impossible to count. If one looks at the complexities of the human anatomy, and how it operates on a daily basis, one cannot imagine the thousand of different functions that occur within the body of a human being at the same time in an autonomous fashion. This can only be construed as a major blessing of love.

God promises to bless His children with kindness and compassion. God will bless all of His children with mercy and love, more than the believer will ever know.

The Promise of Special Blessing

The scripture teaches us in the book of Ephesians; *"But God Who is rich in mercy, because of His great love with which He loved us, even when we were dead in trespasses, made us alive together with Christ by grace you have been saved."* **(Ephesians 2:4-5)**

The believer should always express his concerns for the needs of others. This is an act of love, for God will reward a seed sown to help others.

"You shall surely give to him, and your heart should not be grieved when you give to him, because for this thing the Lord Your God will bless you in all your works and in all to which you put your hand." **(Deuteronomy 15:10)**

Jesus is the only one who can give abundant life to the believer. The abundant life not only means life in its abundance, but living life in its fullness of the blessings of God. Jesus said I am the way, the truth and the life. The believer who is abiding in Jesus and Jesus in him truly has an abundant life.

The bible teaches us in **Deuteronomy 28:8;** *"The Lord will command the blessing on you in your storehouses and in all to which you set your hand, and He will bless you in the land which the Lord your God is giving you."*

The righteous believer can expect many blessings to come upon his life, because the scripture teaches us in the book of **Matthew 7:11;** *"If you then, being evil, know how to give good gifts (blessings) to your children, how much more will your Father Who is in heaven give good things (blessings) to those who ask Him!"*

The believer has the right to ask God for His best, if he is abiding in God and God's word is abiding in him. It gives God pleasure to give His children what they ask. Providing the things they ask for are in the will of God.

You should always think and reflect on the many blessings that you may be enjoying in your life now. For example, your body consists of many muscles, tendons, nerves, cells, bones, etc., that work together to maintain your health.

It is only the blessing of God that causes all the parts of your body to operate the way God intended it to operate.

The bible teaches us in **Psalm 139:14a;** *"I will praise You, for I am fearfully and wonderfully made."*

The believer must realize that he was blessed the day he was born with a magnificent body perfected by God the Almighty. If anyone ever says he is not blessed by God he has not considered the thousands of functions that work in harmony every minute in his own body.

A PROMISE OF A LONG LIFE TO THE BELIEVER

"So if you walk in My ways, to keep My statutes and My commandments, as your father David walked, then I will lengthen your days." **(1 Kings 3:14)**

A long and healthy life is what most people would like to have. God has promised that He would bless the believer with honor and a long life when he obeys His commands.

The scripture teaches us that: *"He shall call upon Me and I will answer him; I will be with him in trouble; I will deliver him and honor him. With long life I will satisfy him, and show him My salvation."* **(Psalm 91:15-16)**

The Promise of Special Blessing

A Promise To Watch Over The Believer

God sees us as dear children who are very limited in what we know about the unknown. We have no knowledge about tomorrow or the future. That is why we must always depend on God for assistance. The bible tells us in the book of John that without Christ we cannot do anything. God knows what we have need of and He has made it clear that He will always be there for us and that He will always watch over us. This promise is one of the most comforting and assuring promises of the bible. It is also a promise of protection and coverage that every believer needs.

We must always remember that God has placed requirements on the believer in order to receive His promises. The believer must always be in obedience to the word of God and totally committed to Him.

"The Lord is near to all who call upon Him, To all who call upon Him in truth. He will fulfill the desire of those who fear Him; He also will hear their cry and save them. The Lord preserves all who love Him, But all the wicked He will destroy." **(Psalm 145:18-20)**

A Promise To Preserve The Believer

The living word of God is Jesus Himself, and in Him is life. Without Him there is no life, for He is the only Way to life itself. He came to this earth that man may have life and have it more abundantly. For Jesus is our life, hope and our peace. Without Him there is only mere existence for man on the earth. Peace can only come from God.

It is one of the fruits of the Spirit. Jesus holds the key to all peace.

147

GOD'S PROMISES

For the believer who is abiding in Jesus, and Jesus is abiding in him, there can be much fruit in his life. This fruit is peace, joy and happiness that surpasses all understanding.

Only God can preserve the life of mortal man. Man cannot preserve his own life.

The scripture teaches us in **Psalm 16:11;** *"You will show me the path of life; in Your presence is fullness of joy; at Your right hand are pleasures forevermore."*

God's word tells the believer whose hope is in the Lord, to be of good courage, and He shall strengthen his heart.

Man cannot successfully guide himself through life without God. One of the greatest unknowns of man is the future, and it is the wise man who seeks God daily to guide him.

The scripture teaches us in **Psalm 48:14;** *"For this is God, our God forever and ever; He will be our guide even to death."*

God desires that His children live a life that is free from worry and burdens. He knows that there is no peace and joy in the believers life if he is carrying many burdens. God has made a way for the believer to be free of all his burdens. His word tells us in **Psalm 55:22;** *"Cast your burden on the Lord, and He shall sustain you; He shall never permit the righteous to be moved."*

God will always find a way to prevent disaster and trouble from overtaking the believer's life. He will show the believer that He can bless him even when trouble and turmoil is at his neighbor's door who does not trust in God.

Scripture teaches us in **Psalm 5:12;** *"For You, O Lord, will bless the righteous; with favor You will surround him as with a shield."*

The Promise of Special Blessing

A PROMISE THAT GOD'S LOVE IS PERFECTED IN US

"No one has seen God at anytime. If we love one another, God abides in us and His love has been perfected in us." (**1 John 4:12**)

"God is love, and he who abides in love abides in God and God in him. Love has been perfected among us in this; that we may have boldness in the day of judgment; because as He is, so are we in this world." (**John 4:16b -17**)

A PROMISE TO KEEP THE BELIEVER YOUNG

Everyone wants to stay young in body and appearance. God knows how to keep the believer young and vibrant. God can keep the believer young for many years. In the old days, God allowed people on the earth to live over nine hundred years and longer. So God knows how to prolong youth in the believers life.

The scripture teaches us, *"God who Crowns you with loving kindness and tender mercies, Who satisfies your mouth with good things, so that your youth is renewed like the eagle."* (**Psalm 103:4b-5**)

We also learn in the book of Isaiah that God blesses the believer who waits on Him for the promises.

"But those who wait on the Lord shall renew their strength; they shall mount up with wings like eagles, they shall run and not be weary, they shall walk and not faint." (**Isaiah 40:31**)

The word of the Lord teaches the believer that God has the power to make our bodies like new at any time He desires. God knows how to keep our bodies young and vibrant for His work.

GOD'S PROMISES

God has promised the believer that when the trials of life come, He will cause all things to work together for our good.

We must always acknowledge Him in everything we do and He will direct us and keep us on the right path. God always knows the right path to take because He knows the future and He knows the purpose and plans He has for each of us.

"And we know that all things work together for good to those who love God, to those who are called according to His purpose." **(Romans 8:28)**

God has promised those who love Him, that He would exalt them and set them on high.

The Believer Can Call On God In Time Of Trouble

Jesus has said there would be trouble in this world; and we can look around us and see that Jesus was right. There is trouble lurking everywhere in every city in America.

In the book of John it tells us; *"These things I have spoken to you, that in Me you may have peace. In the world you will have tribulation; but be of good cheer, I have overcome the world."* **(John 16:33)**

No one is immune to trouble, but the believer has the promises of God to rely on. In **Psalm 46:1** it tells us; *"God is our refuge and strength, a very present help in trouble."*

God's word assures us that we do not have to worry about the consequences of trouble. This scripture in **Psalm 138:7** says; *"Though I walk in the midst of trouble, You will revive me."*

A True Story: The American Officer Who Called On God

During the Vietnam war there were American soldiers who were captured and held as prisoners of war. There was one American officer who was summoned to appear before a Vietnam officer who was acting as a judge on the battlefield. This judge sentenced the American officer to be executed by a five man firing squad. They placed the American officer in front of the firing squad and the five men were told to load their AK 47 rifles with magazine clips filled with ammunition. The firing squad was ordered to fire by the Vietnam commander. As the American officer stood silently by watching the firing squad, in desperation, he earnestly uttered these words to himself in a whisper; "God, I need Your help!" The next sound that the American officer heard was; "click, click, click, click, click!"

Not one of the 5 rifles was able to fire a round of ammunition, for God had answered the officers prayer and caused all 5 rifles to malfunction. The American officer silently laughed for he knew that God had heard his prayer and was with him.

A True Story: I Could Have Been Killed

This incident happened on March 17, 2004 around 9:00 p.m. The bible tells us in **Acts 2:21**; *"And it shall come to pass; that whoever shall call on the name of the Lord shall be saved."*

It was eight thirty in the evening and I was driving about sixty-five miles per hour south on Interstate 285. I was heading home from a meeting and was in a hurry because I had told my wife I would be home in about 20 minutes or less.

I was not completely focused on the next exit which was Interstate 85 south when suddenly I realized that I had almost passed my exit. I tried to make the correction by quickly moving into the median to pick up the exit. In my attempt, I hit several large potholes that I did not even see because it was dark. The potholes were much too deep for my car tires so the impact caused my car to go out of control to the point of almost flipping the car over. I looked out of the left side of the car and I could see the ground and that I was about to have a serious accident! I thought about being crushed in the car. The car was completely out of control! All of this happened so quickly that I did not even have time to pray so I cried out; "Jesus, Jesus save me!" The very next second, some great force settled the car and brought it under control! I knew that God had saved me from having a serious accident! I continued home thanking God for saving me. I am a witness that God will hear the believer's cry for help when they call on Him.

When I arrived home and told my wife about what happened, she said that God impressed on her heart to pray for my safety at the exact same time that I hit the potholes. Our God is AWESOME!

A True Story: God Caused the Lioness to Let Go

In 1999 in Tanzania, Africa, a park ranger named Sidney was riding his bike to work when he suddenly heard the roar of a lion on the road ahead of him. He decided to avoid the lion that was on his trail by taking a short cut to his job. As he was traveling to his job, he noticed that there were two lioness following him. Before he knew it, one of the lioness jumped on him and knocked him off his bike. He ran through the woods and one of the lioness caught up with him and jumped on him again. He cried out to God to save him and miraculously the lioness left him alone. He stated; "it is simple to ask God for help."

A True Story: Attacked by a Mountain Lion

Five young people were hiking in southern California in a wooded area. The group went one and a half miles into the wooded area. There was a small lake ahead about a hundred feet away.

One of the hikers decided to return to the car so she took the same trail back. On the way back in approximately three minutes she was face to face with a mountain lion. She was very frightened and prayed to God to not let the lion kill her.

When the lion attacked her she screamed very loud and the other four hikers heard. The lion was on top of the hiker and was mauling her. The four hikers were able to get the lion away from the injured hiker. She was taken to the hospital and treated for her injuries. God heard her prayers and did not allow the lion to kill her.

A True Story: A Church That Was Facing Foreclosure

A pastor of a small church called a meeting with his staff to pray about the church pending foreclosure. The church had been given the bad news of a foreclosure the day before by the bank.

The pastor ordered the secretary not to interrupt the staff meeting for any reason. The church was behind in mortgage payments in the amount o $250,000 and had exhausted all of its resources but still could not come up with the amount needed to stop the foreclosure. At the meeting the pastor suggested that each staff member should in turn say a prayer and ask God for help. Each member prayed when it was his turn. One of the members had a somewhat different prayer request to God. He asked God to sell some of His cattle on the hill that He owned and provide the church with the funds to stop the foreclosure.

While the meeting was still in process a man entered the church and asked the secretary to see the pastor. The secretary told the man that the pastor was in a meeting and was not to be disturbed. The man told the secretary that he had a donation of $250,000 for the pastor. The secretary thought that the donation was a good enough reason to interrupt the meeting so she led the man into the meeting to speak with the pastor. The man looked at the pastor and said that he was a cattle rancher and he had just left the county fair where he had sold some cattle. He stated that God had directed him to come to this church and give the proceeds of $250,000. The pastor thanked the man and received the $250,000 to stop the foreclosure. The church staff witnessed the power of prayer and how God can come to the aid of those who call upon Him.

A Promise Of God To Give His Children The Best Of Everything

The bible tells us that God is able to give good gifts and good things to His children. **(Matthew 7:11)**

God is our Father Who desires to give us His best, and it pleases Him to do this. It also gives Him pleasure to see His children get excited when they receive from Him. There is no earthly father who can out give God. It is not possible. God has given man the capacity to desire, to love and to have hope.

He indeed knows how to satisfy our desires for gifts and things on this earth. God wants His children to have the best of everything. This includes houses, cars, furniture, clothes, jewelry, food, etc.

In **Isaiah 1:19** the scripture tells us: *"If you are willing and obedient you shall eat the good of the land."*

I must tell you that there are conditions to all of God's promises. First of all, we must commit our lives to the service of God. We must love Him with everything in us. He must have 'first place' in our hearts and lives. We must begin to seek Him continuously. We must always share our wealth with the poor. We must love others as God has loved us. And if we ever forget everything that is required of us by God, we can keep this one thing in mind: *"Fear God and keep His commandments, for this is the conclusion of all that is expected of every child of God."* (**Ecclesiastes 12:13**)

"If they obey and serve Him; they shall spend their days in prosperity and their years in pleasure." (**Job 36:11**)

Chapter Eighteen:

The Promise to Those

Who Trust God

GOD'S PROMISES

THE BELIEVER WILL NEVER BE ASHAMED

BY TRUSTING GOD

There may be many different reasons why a believer may not place his full trust in God. It could be that his faith may be too low or no faith at all. The bible tells us that we only need the faith of a mustard seed and that would be sufficient. God said in His word that we can trust Him to do what He says. If we truly trust God's word, He will always come through for the believer. This we can always count on -- not sometimes but all times. God will always come through for us, if we only believe His word and trust Him. He may not come at the moment we want Him to, but He will come through at the moment He designates to be the right time. God controls people, situations and even time. There is nothing in this vast universe that God cannot control. He made everything and He surely can control everything. The more the believer gets to know God, the more he trusts God. The more the believer experiences the things of God through trials and tribulations, the greater is his faith. I believe that God allows us to go through trials just to increase our faith. Mountain moving faith, I believe is the highest level of faith and the only way I know to have that kind of faith is to have many experiences with trials and tests from God. The more tests, and the more trials we go through, the greater is our faith if we hold on to His promise that He will always be there with us. The bottom line is, do you trust Him?

I have never heard a believer say: "I was trusting in the Lord and He let me down" or "He didn't come through for me". In the book of **Romans 10:11** it tells us; *"Anyone who trusts in Him will never be put to shame."*

To trust God unconditionally one must know Him. To know God one must invest time reading and studying the word of God. At times, the believer will find it necessary to consult with the Holy Spirit for understanding of what he is reading.

158

The Promise to Those Who Trust God

In time, the believer will know God and trusting Him will be easy because a relationship will develop between God and the believer by way of the Holy Spirit.

Chapter Nineteen:

The Summary Of God's Promises

GOD'S PROMISES

THE SUMMARY OF GOD'S PROMISES

There may be several reasons why God has made promises to His followers. One reason that stands out as to why God promised His child so much is that every promise requires faith. However, without the promises there would be no need to exercise faith. Even our hope is based on the promises of God. For what would we hope for if we did not have the promises of God. Without hope we would not have the desire to live the life God intended us to live. The promises of God are His expressions of love and concern for His followers.

Someone has stated that there are over 4000 promises in the bible. Some of the promises in the bible are explicit while others are implied. An implied promise may be revealed by the Holy Spirit, whereas an explicit promise is evident by the context of the words of the promise itself.

God's love for His followers is revealed through the promises He has made to His followers. The promises of God give the believer something to live for. Why? We know that God's word is true and His promises are His word. God's word can always be trusted. The bible tells us that God's word will always stand.

God requires the believer to wait on the manifestation of the promises. Our faith will grow as we wait on the promises of God to be revealed in our lives. Our faith cannot grow until it is tested and tried. Waiting on the promises of God will test our faith. If our faith is weak we may not continue to wait on God to manifest a promise in our life. We must remember that God is the Author and Finisher of our faith.

Everything that the believer needs or desires is contained in the promises of God. However, God wants us to depend on Him for everything that we will ever need or desire. He wants His children to operate in faith to receive from Him.

The Summary Of God's Promises

Throughout this book I have shared true stories that demonstrate the power of faith that people relied on to bring God into their circumstances when they needed Him. God has promised that He will come to the aid of a follower in time of need. All the follower has to do is to call on the name of the Lord and God will help Him. God will at times help a person who is in trouble even when he is not a believer because of His mercy and grace. However, He never made a promise to an unsaved person that He would always be there to help in time of a life and death situation. God only made this promise to His children.

God knows that His children have needs and desires. God wants His children to have all things that are good for them in His view. God wants to be the only source for everything that the believer will ever need or desire. I believe that this is the second reason that God has made promises to His children.

We must never forget that God's promises are not 'free'. There is a price that must be paid by every believer. We must allow God to train us. The believer will often cry out to God to stop the affliction. He may at times even think of the training as punishment, but it is not. It is an act of God's uncompromising love to change our character.

Our training begins with God shaping, molding, and refining our character to become like Jesus. During this period of training, suffering and affliction will occur, but God will see us through all the pain that must come while we are in the furnace of affliction. It is for the good of the believer to go through this training. No character can be changed for better without suffering. We must remember that any pain or suffering that comes to us in our training from God is also managed by Him. In other words, there is a limit of pain and suffering which is controlled by the love of God Himself. We must always remember that the bible is a book of instructions for the believer to live by. It teaches us how to love God and our neighbor. It also teaches us that everything we do for others must be done in love. If there is an order of things we must do after we are saved, it would be the experience of seeking the kingdom of God.

We must never forget that there is no success without God, for He is the source of all success. If you want to get close to the heart of God as a servant, then consider the needs of the poor and the unfortunate. Have a heart for those who cannot help themselves. When you do this, you are favoring God's righteous cause. God gives four (4) things to those who please Him: wisdom, knowledge, joy, and wealth which is a blessing that is found in **Ecclesiastes 2:26.**

And finally, all wealth belongs to God. When He blesses us with wealth, we should keep in mind that He expects us to be good stewards and see to it that some of the wealth is used to advance His kingdom here on earth. This is a sure way to please God and expect His best in our lives.

Epilogue:

GOD'S PROMISES

It is God's will for His children to experience the best that life has to offer, so He made promises to them. Every promise that God made serves as a special blessing in the life of the believer. The blessing of every promise is God's best for the believer on this earth. God further demonstrated His love to the world by sending His son to die for the sins of the world. His promises are for those who have accepted His Son as their Savior. The reason God made promises to His children is quite simple; He loves His children. The promises are designed to encourage, to strengthen, and to give hope. Before any believer receives a single promise from God, God must prepare him for the promise. Every believer will not agree to this preparation from God. Some believers will say yes and some will say no to this training. Consequently, those who refuse the training eliminate themselves from the promises of God.

It is God's will that every believer come into His rest after salvation. This is the place where all of the promises of God are available. God's promise are like a lifeline to the believer in his daily living. During the period of seeking the Kingdom of God, He will refine, mold, and enhance the character of every believer. After this phase of training is completed, God will bring the believer into a period of waiting. This phase of the training is designed to develop patience, trust, self-control, and a dependence on God. This stage of the training process is the most difficult of all because God is operating in full control of our lives and the believer is being tested for his ability to trust God and just wait on Him. After the waiting period, God moves the believer into the promise land. There is no physical promise land today like it was for the Israelites in the Old Testament. Today's promise land is the promises of God, which are better and more superior than the promise land of old.

To bring a promise of God into the life of a believer, the believer must apply what he has learned during the period of preparation. However, God has already given the victory to the believer to manifest the promise. The believer must believe, claim, and stand on the promise. Storms and other opposition will occur to try to move the believer from standing on a promise. God will assist the believer to stand and not move from the promise. The believer has been trained to seek God for help in making the promise a reality. God will give the believer victory because He promised He would.

The final stage in seeking the Kingdom of God is God's rest. It is the place where God takes care of all the needs of the believer. The days of toiling and struggling have ended. All of God's promises are available just for the asking. None of the promises of God can fail because they are the word of God.

The promises of God have unlimited value. All the gold and silver in the earth cannot match the value of God's promises. God designed His promises to give His children hope, joy, peace and contentment. There is no greater joy for the believer to experience than to meditate on the promises of God. He should reflect on the promises and use them as a daily guide to live the life God intended him to live. Not one day should go by without us reflecting on the goodness of God and giving Him thanks for all He has promised. And finally, think for a moment of what the world has to offer and think for a moment all that God has promised to those who love Him.

If you do not have Jesus in your life, I pray that you make the decision today to accept Him as your Savior and Lord. **Romans 10:9 NIV** says, *"That if you confess with your mouth Jesus is Lord and believe in your heart that God raised Him from the dead you will be saved."*

About the Author

Odell Young, Jr. has authored several books: Only God Can Give You the Power to Get Wealth, Real Estate Investing for the Beginners, and Getting Started In Real Estate.

Odell was called into the ministry in October of 2007. The training he has received came by way of the Holy Spirit through Michael Coley, an apostle of God. Odell has been in training for over 4 years, since the conception of this book.

In October of 2007, God had not yet not revealed what kind of ministry He wanted Odell to be involved in. However, after 3 years, it was obvious that God had the role of an apostle in store for him.

God has since called Odell to advance the body of Christ with the knowledge of the word of God. He has been called to assist and enhance pastors teaching the word of God, to create a plan to help feed the poor across the world, and to help finance the teaching of God's word through the church. In Hosea 4:6 the bible teaches that God's children are perishing for the lack of knowledge. Odell believes that the primary information the body of Christ is lacking is the knowledge and understanding of the promises of God.

Odell is a graduate of Morehouse College with a degree in Business Administration. He and his wife Delores reside in Palmetto, Georgia. They have been blessed with 3 children, Angela, DeAnn and Kevin.

In the fall of October 2007, God revealed to Odell that he had been doing business the world's way rather than God's way. His third book, ***Only God Can Give You the Power to Get Wealth,*** is the outcome of his relationship with God, and spiritual journey into new business ventures—doing God's work and getting wealth God's way.

Discover what may be blocking your blessings!

This book is a "how to" guide for you, a believer, to become empowered to gain wealth. The best way to build wealth is to build it God's way. In fact, it is the only way.

As you develop your relationship with Him, you will be empowered to accomplish that which you pursue. After all, God is the one who ultimately decides if you will receive all that He has promised (including love, goodness, kindness, blessings, protection from danger, peace, good health, money and God's mercy). He also determines if you will keep that which He gives so freely. "Remember," says Mr. Young, "It is God who gives the believer the power to get wealth. When God gives you wealth, He adds no trouble to it."

For speaking engagements or to order copies:

Email: **odell.youngjr@gmail.com**

Call: **404-319-0913**

Mail: **P.O. Box 801**
Palmetto, Ga. 30268

ISBN-10: 0-615-31158-6
ISBN-13: 978-0-615-31158-6

Notes

Notes